OUR BOY

ALWAYS A COLDSTREAMER

The Battles of the Rhineland and
North-West Germany in 1945

The life of a Coldstream Guardsman and
his family at home during the battles of the
Rhineland and North-West Germany in 1945

GRAHAM PHILIP DIX

Troubador Publishing Ltd
Unit E2 Airfield Business Park
Harrison Road, Market Harborough
Leicestershire LE16 7UL
Tel: 0116 279 2299
Email: books@troubador.co.uk
Web: www.troubador.co.uk

ISBN 978 1 80514 422 9

British Library Cataloguing in Publication Data.
A catalogue record for this book is available from the British Library.

Printed and bound in Great Britain by 4edge Limited
Typeset in 11pt Minion Pro by Troubador Publishing Ltd, Leicester, UK

Dedicated to my nan – Lillian Annie Amelia Bateman
also, my mum – Iris Sarah Dix
and my aunties and uncles – Kenneth, Gordon, Hazel,
Mary, and Vera

To 2667147 Guardsman Basil R Bateman

'You have joined a Regiment whose reputation is indeed as our motto implies 'Second to None' I hope you will always be proud of this just as the Regiment is proud of all those who have played their part in building up this reputation, to which, I do not doubt, you yourself will contribute during your course of your Service. The characteristics that go to make a 'Coldstreamer' in the best sense of the word, are not the monopoly of any one class or any one calling. Rich men and poor men, townsmen and country men, men from the factory, men from the farm, have all added something to the lustre of the Coldstream Star. I would like you to realise too, that it is not merely as a result of exploits on the field of battle that the reputation of the Coldstream stands so high. There are many other qualities that go to make a good Coldstreamer – qualities which the nation will need to the utmost after the war. Remember that the Coldstream is not only a Regiment of the Army- it is also a family in which the welfare of each one of the members and their dependants, both during and after service with the Regiment, is always a matter of interest to those responsible for administering the Regiment.

I hope you will be happy in the comradeship of the Regiment and that you will bear in mind the old saying 'Once a Coldstreamer always a Coldstreamer'

Lieutenant-Colonel Commanding Coldstream Guards

Contents

Prologue

Mr Farrant answered the telephone call on the fourth ring. He could tell it was from a pay phone from the familiar clunking and whirring noise as the coins were being inserted by the caller. He recognised the caller immediately and looked across the room at his wife with that look that caused her to get out of her chair and come to listen at the earpiece. Together they listened to Lillian as she painfully relayed her saddest of news, trying to sound sufficiently poised given he was Basil's employer, but her voice wavered as she forced back the tears. He had been expecting the call as he had insisted that he be contacted when she was ready to come home. The news wasn't totally unexpected but still came as a shock.

He was a good man and jumped to making the arrangements to collect her from Shaftesbury. He checked the weather forecast as the past few days had seen overnight frost and temperatures below zero during the days, making for difficult driving conditions, particularly for a relatively long journey. The forecast for today was 'unsettled but milder', better still take a couple of car blankets. He knew the route there from his anxious and stressful trip just three weeks before, but he checked it anyway as there were several options. Should he go Wantage, Lambourne, Marlborough, Devizes way, to avoid going through Swindon? He pondered this but decided that going Swindon way last time was direct and the road was good. He did the normal checks for a longish journey and set off with a flask and his map book.

He found her waiting in the Hospital Reception building, which was no more than a low hastily erected wooden structure similar to all the other buildings, making an austere first impression for visitors. He rather awkwardly offered his condolences, picked up her meagre suitcase and saw her to the car, he holding her arm, she lost in silence. He helped her into the Wolseley as all gentlemen did, seating her in the rear and offering her a car blanket which she accepted. The journey home through glorious countryside seemed almost two dimensional in the dullness created by low cloud threatening rain. The three hour journey was one of deep sadness and little conversation.

Lillian's thoughts turned to seeing Basil walk into the house a couple of weeks before Christmas, in his service uniform. The euphoria at seeing and hugging him for the first time in many months, the relief at knowing her youngest son had survived unscathed, soon turned to anguish as she stood back and looked at him. He looked so dreadfully thin and gaunt. She thought of the concern on Dr Dempsey's face as he examined him the following day and his insistence on immediate admission to the Radcliffe Infirmary. She saw a flash of the telegram from Shaftesbury Military Hospital. 'Placed on the dangerously ill list' it had said. She thought of seeing him in the hospital bed for the first time, the clean white sheets, his pale face breaking into a faint smile when he saw her enter the ward.

She noticed a signpost indicating Oxford was 10 miles away, the recognition that the journey was nearing its end jolting her back to the here and now, she remembered that Mr Farrant had left a bag of potatoes just inside the gate a few days before her leaving. He had often helped out in this manner whilst Basil had been on Active Service, leaving various seasonal produce and milk by the gate. She thanked him for that, which generated a brief discussion about the state of the rationing before drifting back into silence with just the sound of the wind rushing through the badly fitting doors, the roar of the engine and whine of the gearbox in the lower gears.

Her mind drifted back to the Hospital. Basil was in Ward 11. She had been able to nurse and fuss over him during the day and had befriended other mothers of the poor boys in the ward. She thought of Mrs Williams from Truro whose son, Garfield, passed away two days before Basil in the bed next to him. The thought of nursing briefly reminded her of the Canadian Soldier amputee she had nursed during the last war. He had asked her to marry him. Her mind lured her back to the moment Basil drifted into final unconsciousness; she was holding his hand as his grip loosened.

Once back at the house he helped her indoors, setting her case down just inside the door. She thanked him and closed the door. It was late afternoon and the tea for the household needed making. Iris and Vera were inside with Hazel looking after them. Mary would be home from work soon. There were no more tears to cry and the needs of the family occupied her thoughts till night time. Little was said about Basil. All the children knew what had happened and could sense that Lillian was struggling to stay composed just as she did when Vera was still a toddler and George had died. Only Vera asked about him and Lillian merely said, "he is with God now".

Once all were in bed she carried his army issue bag into her room. It had been propped up in the corner of the small room that had been his room he shared with Vera before joining up. She took the gold signet ring she had given to him on his last leave out of her purse and laid it on the bed. It had been a gift for his nineteenth birthday as he had so wanted one just like all his friends had. She had saved for weeks to be able to buy it. The hospital orderly had taken it off Basil's finger at her request and she had wrapped it in her handkerchief. From his army bag she took out his fearsome looking bayonet, in its leather scabbard and laid it on the bed. Next his combat knife in its leather sheaf. She shuddered and placed it next to the bayonet. His green beret was on top of the other service uniform. She folded it in her hands and pressed it to her face. The cap badge had been polished so much that the cross in the centre was barely visible. She pulled the pin from behind the badge, reassembled it and laid it beside the ring. She removed the service uniform and folded it for later return to whoever required it. At the bottom of the bag she saw his pocket watch. Gently holding its leather pouch in one hand she removed it and studied the weighty slender object. Its black face with luminous hands and digits stared back at her. She gave it a gentle wind and heard it ticking powerfully. As she placed it back into its wallet she noticed another cap badge in the corner of the bag, this one brand new. She stood on a chair on the landing and slipped the bayonet and knife into the loft, she didn't want Iris or Vera playing with such dangerous weapons. Gathering up the treasured items from the bed she went to her room and laid them on her drawer unit. From a drawer she carefully picked out a collection of opened letters held together with a rubber band; the letters Basil had sent to her throughout his time away. She opened the last one he had sent her and read it.

"Dear Mother, many thanks for your most welcome letter which I have just received. Also, I wish to thank you for the parcel which I received two days ago. My friend and I had a good tuck in of chocolate and apples."

She smiled at this thought.

"I guessed you would be surprised to hear from me again so soon.................. We had a big parade this morning to welcome the colours back to the battalion, after the parade we marched past the division's commander. The only thing I did not like was that I was very cold. My fingers were numb after we had stood to attention for about fifteen minutes. It does not matter about the photographs for now, we will try to get some taken when I am on leave.......... Well mother this is all the news for now so I will close, cherio for now, Your loving son Basil xxxxxxx xxxxxxxxxx.

She loved to see all those kisses. All the letters ended with lots of kisses. The mention of the photographs prompted her to reach into the drawer and pick up a small mirror with a black and white photograph on the rear. Basil had sent it, explaining that it had been free with the other photographs he had developed. He hadn't thought they were very good. She picked up those four small photographs with ragged edges which seemed to be a feature of that particular developer as opposed to being ripped or cut that way. The first one showed a man in uniform stood inside the ruins of Cologne Cathedral. Basil had said in one of the letters that the 'Yank' had walked into the picture just as he took it. The next was of him with his bicycle stood next to a pretty girl of his age. He had mentioned her as 'the fraulein' in a previous letter, writing that she had gone to the 'Russian Sector' just before the 5th Battalion disbanded and she wouldn't know how to find him when she returned. How could she tell her about Basil? How would she ever know? She placed all of these infinitely precious keepsakes in her jewellery box and closed the draw. She quietly cried herself to sleep.

Some days later a letter arrived from the Guards Headquarters in London. She opened it expecting the content. It read,

'Dear Madam, it is with deep regret that I send you an official Army Form to-day, notifying you of the death of your son. I wish to express on my own behalf, and on behalf of the Coldstream Guards, my sincere sympathy in your bereavement. I hope you may be comforted by the fact that he was doing his duty on behalf of his King and Country, and that he will be much missed by his comrades in the Regiment. If you are in any difficulties at any time, I hope you will communicate with these Headquarters, we will always help or advise you to the best of our ability'.

The funeral took place the following week under unsettled

skies, the weather was mild for the end of January, but coats and gloves were still needed. The Coldstream Guards had offered to provide a fully paid funeral with Military Honours, but her thoughts were of bitterness towards the Guards. She knew from Basil's letters that he was sick of the pomp, the continuous polishing and general life associated with being in the 1st Battalion Coldstreams in peacetime. The Guards Battalion he joined and loved, the 'Fighting Fifths' was gone. His friends he trusted his life to had been posted far and wide. The thought of the haunting, desperately sad sound of a Guardsman performing the 'last post' reverberating around the graveyard at Cumnor Church was too much for her. Instead, she opted to have Basil interred in her husband George's grave, 'My Georgie' she called him when she talked about him. That at least gave her some comfort. Family and friends attended the small gathering. Flowers adorned the grave.

I

Introduction

'Lillian' is my grandmother. Lillian Annie Amelia Bateman or 'nan' to me. She lived with us, or rather we lived with her, as my parents married and lived at her house and ended up jointly purchasing the house with her from the council. As a consequence, my nan played a major part in my upbringing.

She was of the generation that had to endure two world wars, the first in her early twenties and the second as a widow with seven children. She had experienced the harshness of being brought up with strict Victorian values, life in 'service' as a teenager, and the relative poverty of working folk of the time. She had taken in washing, worked as a part time 'nanny' for rich folk in the village and cleaned the church, all with no other financial support. There was no 'welfare state' back then. She had faced the trauma of her eldest son, my Uncle Kenneth, being wounded in North Africa and the unbearable weight of losing her youngest son when he should have been safe. The war had ended and all the people on active service were in the process of being demobbed and returning home.

Basil is my Uncle whom I never met. All my life I have known about him, and I am told that I am very much like him. As a primary school pupil, I used to attend St Michael's Church in Cumnor on St George's Day, Easter, and Harvest Festival. I remember being so proud as I looked up at the organ pipes with his name printed there commemorating the war dead. I walked past the War Memorial on the way to and from school, often glancing at his name on the left-hand side, just to check it was still there. I attended most Remembrance Sunday Services around the memorial in my school years and even attended as the local police officer in later years to lay a wreath and to 'police' the parade. On many occasions in my younger years, I cut the grass on his grave with hand shears and have visited his grave most years. Although unmarked he is buried with my grandfather George Bateman who died in 1939 just before the war broke out. Basil's headstone is of white marble and of the standard type used by the Commonwealth War Graves Commission the world over, making it instantly recognisable in the lower graveyard to the right of the church. The gravestone is inscribed:

2667147 Guardsman B. R. Bateman Coldstream Guards 22nd January 1946 Age 19 'One of the Bravest One of the best God grant him now Eternal rest'.

Every year without fail one member of the family places a wreath on his grave at Christmas time. At first it was my nan, as she grew old my dad took over, and now my sister Pauline has taken over for the family.

I have always been aware of the photo of Basil in his uniform now on the cover of this book. It is of the type all servicemen have officially taken, to ensure the family have a quality picture of their loved one in the event of their death in service of their country. The black and white photograph, now faded to sepia, taken under studio lighting shows a very young man of eighteen years old with a handsome face, looking slightly to the right of the camera with a faint smile. He has black wavy hair parted in the middle as per the fashion at the time. I have stared so many times at this photograph and wondered about what happened to him, how he died, and what he did in the war. Over the years I have asked more questions than I have ever had answers for. The plain fact was that he died without ever really telling anyone 'at home' any detail of what he did or what he saw during his time on active service. This was the way it was back then; no one wanted their loved ones back home to worry about them. Everything was downplayed. The only concrete information I knew was that Basil was in the Coldstream Guards and spent the last year of the war in Germany and that he died in January 1946 some eight months after the war ended as a result of an infection he caught whilst in Germany. The family widely believed that he caught the infection whilst guarding German SS guards made to bury the dead bodies in Belsen Concentration Camp after it was liberated in April 1945, this information coming most likely from nan's conversations with him whilst in the military hospital and whilst he was on leave.

The 'precious keepsakes' my nan kept so carefully have always been, and will always be, a part of my life. Some months before my marriage she produced a box containing those precious items. First, she gave me Basil's gold signet ring and asked that I use it as my wedding ring. She then produced the pocket watch in its leather case together with Basil's two service medals and two cap badges. She wanted me to have them and care for them as she had done for all those years. I promised to do just that and asked if she would mind if I had my initials engraved on the ring. She liked that idea, and I subsequently had my initials 'GPD' engraved in time for the wedding.

Basil's medals were sent to my nan sometime after his death. They are the France and Germany Star and the 1939-45 War Medal. I believe he was also entitled to the 1939-45 Star but that has either been mislaid over the years or was never issued. All are commemorative medals issued to all those who served in those theatres of war.

Basil had worked on a farm close by from age 14 years until his call up at age 18 years. I also worked on that farm years later in my summer holidays and worked with one of the farm workers, Jack Miller, who had been Basil's workmate and friend. Mr Farrant was the farmer. It is this lifetime of association with Basil, I even slept in the same bedroom as he had, that has intrigued me. However there has always been one overwhelming fact and that is that Basil is the only member of my close family to have been denied a full life and that has always sat heavily with me. There is an injustice there and this has been my driver to somehow put this right, to ensure that Basil is never forgotten. With so little information about him in the family it was difficult to know where to start.

Upon my nan's death the letters, documents and photographs found their way to me. They sat in a drawer for many years before I started reading them. Information contained in these letters and documents proved to be the 'Rosetta Stone' in unlocking and providing an intricate insight into Basil's life from joining the Coldstream Guards to his death on 22nd January 1946. I was able to identify not only his particular battalion but also the company he was in within the battalion, together with confirmation that at key times he was 'there'. Access then to the Battalion's War Diary provided precise locations and details of the battalion's progress through Europe, down to detail of actions by individual companies of men and indeed in some cases, individual men. My mum Iris, and my auntie Vera are the only surviving members of Basil's siblings and they were both very young at the time of Basil's death. Nevertheless, I have asked them to search deep to recall memories of Basil and these memories have been the glue to cement parts of the information together.

Just about everyone is aware of the names of the great battles of WW1 – Somme, Passchendaele, Gallipoli, and of the WW2 battles such as Dunkirk, Arnhem, D–Day and the Battle of the Bulge etc. The film industry has made a selected few battles and exploits forever famous in films such as 'The Longest Day', 'The Bridge at Remagen', 'The Battle of the Bulge', 'Saving Private Ryan' and many more. In researching Basil's war history, I discovered that not only were Basil's war exploits largely unknown to the family, the epic battles he fought in have largely been lost to history too. The battle for the Rhineland for example was arguably the toughest and most bloody of the war on the western front, ending in a decisive victory and disaster for the German forces.

My research has drawn on official documents, his letters and photographs, personal accounts from others, and by retracing his exact steps. Walking the battlefield sites and observing the ground he fought over, together with seeing obvious traces of his presence in the form of bullet and shell holes in buildings, proved an emotional experience.

Here follows then my best attempt at doing justice for Basil, his family, his friends, and the 5th Battalion Coldstream Guards by telling his, and their story as accurately as possible. In doing so I hope to throw light on the battles they fought throughout 1945, now with the knowledge of the 'bigger picture' that they could never have had as Guardsmen. In some cases, I believe these are the most comprehensive accounts to date.

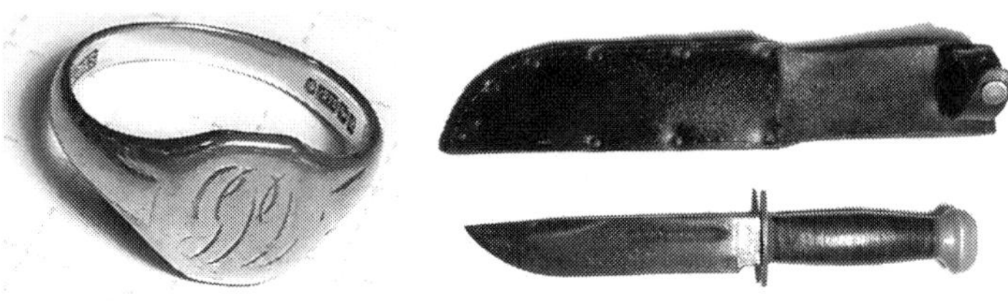

Basil's gold signet ring for his 19th birthday

An identical RH pal 36 knife to Basil's

Cap badges. One almost worn away by polishing

Basil's military issue pocket watch

Basil's medals

2

Impressions of a faraway war

Basil was born in Appleton Road, Cumnor, a small village just outside Oxford city, went to Cumnor School, and then to nearby Botley School for a short time, before working on a farm no more than a mile from his house at the age of fourteen. He was 'country born' like most of the residents of Cumnor in those days, and for the many generations before them. He had probably travelled to Oxford on the bus caught from outside the house a few times, but the village life, home life, and the farm provided the fulfilment he desired. He was a typical young man of his time with good looks and charm. Charm enough at least for Violet Smith to be sweet on him.

Cumnor, as Basil knew it, hadn't been touched by the war, or even air raids, but there were always allied aircraft in the skies above from the local bases such as Stanton Harcourt, Brize Norton, Abingdon, Harwell, Fyfield Wick and the Americans at Grove. One morning a Wellington Bomber was seen, passing low over the village on return from a bombing raid with large parts missing from the tail plane. On another occasion a string of bombs was heard being jettisoned by a German Bomber near Besselsleigh village as it was pursued by Spitfires. On the night of the 14th of November 1940, the villagers could clearly see the night sky in the north being illuminated by the devastating air raid on Coventry, and glimpses through the clouds of hundreds of the attacking German bombers. In 1943 a Spitfire seen by many villagers was performing acrobatics over Bradley Farm when it went into a nose-dive and crashed in a field nearby.

American troops were stationed in the grounds of the school at Besselsleigh. They often walked past the house. Iris was in her early teens at the time and recalls being told off by her elder sister Mary when she chatted to the Americans at the gate. They called her 'Red' on account of her auburn hair, but it was Mary they were interested in.

In the spring of 1944, a mysterious camp was set up which consisted of a large marquee erected in the field not 200 yards from the house. It was manned by a team of six RAF uniformed men who worked and camped there. It became a source of intrigue. Basil would have passed the camp every day to and from work on the farm.

There were many Italian Prisoners of War working on most of the farms in the area and a Prisoner of War Camp at Harcourt Hill near Cumnor Hurst. On one particular occasion, Iris when walking past the Camp with her cousin and looking at the prisoners was alarmed when they all ran to the wire and were shouting at them. The men were just calling out to pretty girls in an amorous way and an armed guard saw their alarm and reassured them that they were safe.

As was the case with every part of the country, evacuees arrived at the outbreak of the war and remained for the duration. These had the effect of throwing the schools into chaos trying to accommodate their education. Many homes in Cumnor took in evacuees, most of which came from Silvertown in East London. They arrived in three coaches at the Village Hall where they were allocated out to homes. The Webb family next door took in one evacuee, a ten year old boy named Alfie Benmore. The Money family on the other side took in three. Their mother used to come and stay there for a few days at a time when she could but was unfortunately killed in the Blitz. The large house across the road took in several. The children there were seen staring out of one of the bedroom windows, gesturing at Farrant's field next to their house and shouting excitedly. They were amazed by the sight of the cows in the field and had no idea what they were.

Basil had left Botley School in 1940 to work on Farrant's farm, a few months after the arrival of the evacuees.

Young men he would have known from school would have been given their 'call up' papers and disappeared off to various armed forces. Looking around he would have seen that he and his best friend Dan from next door were of the very few not in some form of uniform. They talked to each other most evenings at the back of the wash house. Basil's brother, Curly (Gordon) was already away in the RAF, whilst Ken, had joined the Grenadier Guards and had been fighting in North Africa. Ken would have told him some of his experiences of the incredibly tough training and his war experiences in the hands of the Germans. Ken had been shot in the kneecap trying to storm a machine gun post. The Germans had counter-attacked and he was at their mercy. They bandaged his wound and stuck his rifle upright in the sand with his steel helmet on it to warn the tanks not to run him over. He was very thankful for them potentially saving his life and the humane treatment metered out. As an impressionable teenager Basil would have been enthralled by his stories.

Experiences such as these would have been his extremely limited exposure to the war. The inevitable call up papers arriving on his eighteenth birthday were to change all that.

3

Caterham

Lillian knew the human cost of war, as did many young ladies of her time. She had nursed a Canadian soldier who had lost a leg during the Vimy Ridge offensive in 1917 and cycled every day to care for him in a 'pop up' hospital near Cumnor. She would have seen at first hand the hideous wounds they had, missing limbs, blinded, burned, gassed and shell shocked (PTSD we now call it). She knew the young men of Cumnor who never came home.

As a mother she faced the anguish of Ken being wounded in the knee. As soon as she had been told by telegram that Ken was in the John Radcliffe Hospital, she cycled there straight away to see him, getting stopped by a policeman as she cycled straight through a red light. When Basil's 'call up' papers arrived, Lillian did all she could to try and stop him going. At that time there was talk of the allies invading Europe and she certainly wouldn't have wanted Basil anywhere near what she knew would be killing fields like the last war. She had asked Mr Farrant to declare Basil as an essential worker in a reserved occupation but there were always Land Army girls able to take over the men's jobs on farms, so her attempts failed. In the event, although conscripted, Basil must have had a preference to join the Coldstream Guards. Probably influenced by Ken being a Grenadier.

Farm Labourer to Guardsman was going to be a monumental transformation. He was joining the Coldstream Guards and would certainly come to know that and be proud to be a 'Coldstreamer'. The Regiment has an awesome reputation with battle honours at most conflicts fought by Britain ever since their formation during the English Civil War.

On the day he left home to meet the Guards' Recruitment Officer at Oxford Railway Station Lillian will have fussed over him as she always did. He would have had sandwiches packed in his suitcase, along with his clothes; washed and ironed by her. He will have promised to write and to take care of himself and be home as soon as he was allowed. Hazel, the eldest, went on the bus with him to see him off at the station. There was a small group of other recruits assembling there. One was a farmer's son, Mansel Godwin from Weston on the Green, just outside Oxford. His farming background soon led to conversation with Basil and it soon became clear that both were destined to join the Coldstream Guards and to report to Caterham Barracks.

At almost 5' 11" tall and of strong build Basil was a perfect recruit for the Coldstream Guards. He was naturally quiet and unassuming but possessed a warmth that others found alluring and approachable, thus he had no problem making friends and would chat readily to those he felt comfortable around. As a man of his time he knew his place in society and as a farm labourer was naturally subservient to Mr Farrant, the farmer he had worked four years for. His immediate friendship with Mansel, a farmer's son would therefore seem unlikely and must have been perpetuated by them both finding themselves in the same predicament, linked only by the fact that they were both from the Oxford area with a farming background, and needing mutual support in the face of a very uncertain and somewhat frightening future. The ethos of the Coldstream Guards would soon break down any such class barriers amongst Guardsmen but this initial meeting on equal terms between Basil and Mansel gave them some mutual security and a natural bond. There started a close and lasting friendship with Mansel Godwin. Mansel was almost as tall as Basil, just a few months older with rugged good looks and the hint of a profound intelligence. His close set eyes and a wry smile, exuding an air of confidence.

The meeting at Oxford Station must have been an exciting but apprehensive experience for the pair of them. I try to relate to this by remembering my journey to Reading Rail Station to start my training in Thames Valley Police. I sat on the bus laid on to collect us, not knowing anyone. I looked around for potential company and saw a sea of faces looking as apprehensive as me. Some had obviously just left the army and had haircuts so sharp you could slice your finger on. Some looked such tough men I thought I had made a huge mistake. Perhaps Basil and Mansel thought that way too. In any event it was a huge adventure for young men just turned eighteen. How shocked they must have been as the train neared London to see the devastation caused by the Blitz and the V1 Flying Bombs! Basil could have had no concept of what he was to witness in the months to come.

Basil and Mansel arrived at the Coldstream Guards training camp at Caterham in Surrey on Thursday 1st June 1944. Basil was given the Army Number 2667147 and enlisted for the 'duration of the emergency'. His height was recorded as being 5ft 10 3/4" with a 40 ¼" chest, blue eyes, brown hair and weighing 194 lbs. He had passed A1 Fit. His course of inoculations began that day. His paybook was issued a few days later and signed. He designated Dan Money, his next door neighbour (and school friend) as the executor of his Will.

I have a team photograph detailing names of all the young men in Basil's intake which coupled with the collection of letters, was extremely helpful to identify Basil's closest friends throughout his time on active service. In this photograph, his soon to be firm friends are all gathered around him. Guardsman 2667195 Paul Hagan, Guardsman 2667197 George Davidson, Guardsman 26671** Fred Robson and of course Guardsman 2267150 Mansel Godwin, amongst others. They were all assigned to '8 Platoon' of the Training Battalion. Transfer to a forward battalion would come at the end of the training. In my own period of initial training in the police I found that having shoulder (serial) numbers that were numerically close to others around you gave an initial automatic bond. The length of time in training, of helping each other through it, coupled with a knowledge that the final posting would mean remaining together, created a lasting friendship. This seems to be exactly the case for Basil, Mansel, George, Paul, and Fred. A lasting 'Band of Brothers' was forming.

As is often the case with human friendships, one friend emerged as the closest friend and that turned out to be George Davidson. George was again almost as tall as Basil and the girls would have described him as very handsome.

This gave him an air of confidence and a certain cheekiness that made him the character others would want to aspire to. The fact that he looked remarkably similar to Basil may have helped to bond their friendship.

The serious expression exuded a thoughtfulness about Fred Robson. The shortest of the friends but still almost 5' 9". He would go on to demonstrate a caring side as their friendship grew that made him a likeable and loyal friend, as did Paul Hagan. Paul was the most dapper of the friends, even sporting a thin moustache throughout the initial training, surely a difficult feat that required a meticulous air for detail. His dark hair and prominent eyebrows gave him an almost Latin look.

Group photo at Caterham during training. Note that Basil and his friends are all grouped together in the second row

George Davidson

Mansel Godwin

Fred Robson

Paul Hagan

There are no other records of Basil's time at Caterham however a fellow Guardsman – Derrick Jackson experienced the training some time before Basil and provides an excellent insight.[1]

Just like Basil and Mansel he caught the train to London and then on to Caterham. Suitcase in hand he saw the barrack entrance guarded by a 'burly' sergeant. *"I cannot remember the words in large letters over the main gate but if the words had been – Abandon hope all ye who enter here, I would have said later in my training that those words could be applicable".* The new recruits were quickly formed up in groups under the charge of a corporal. They were taken to one of the wooden 'huts' set around a large parade ground that was to become home for a few weeks. On the other side of the parade ground were prison like stone buildings that were the peacetime barracks that were occupied by other recruits more fortunate than them, as they were warm and comfortable, with iron beds. Cases were left in the hut and the group were formed up and marched to the dining room. *"We enjoyed an excellent meal, which would have done credit to any hotel".* Next, they were marched to the Quartermasters Store to be issued their kit. *"It was a forest of equipment, there were rows upon rows of boots, avenues of battle dresses and dozens of shelves, the whole place looked like a huge store back in civvy street".* The group were all each issued with a large blue kitbag and then walked along a line of stalls being issued at each with items of clothing, towels, boots, and various kit. Particular attention was paid to the fit of the trousers and tunics. *"I finished up with my arms full of clothes, towels, boots etc. and once again we marched off".* Next, they were issued with a straw mattress, sheets and bedding. Once back in their wooden hut that could loosely be described as a barracks, they had time to make up their beds, pack away their civilian clothes and finally chat to each other. That concluded day one of their strange new life.

"In the middle of the night, or rather 6.30.a.m. as it really was, the sound of a bugle rang out across the parade ground. Suddenly the hut door burst open and a voice was heard –

Wakey wakey, rise and shine". The person at the door was an experienced trained guardsman assigned to training new recruits and held responsible for the occupants of the hut. Having quickly dressed in record time he formed them up with wash kit under their arms and marched them to the wash house and then on to the mess room. *"The food at Caterham was always good and plentiful, although it was the duty of an officer to ask in the mess hall if there were any complaints. I am sure that there was never any cause for complaint at Caterham"*. Later that day they were issued their regimental numbers.

They were now uniformed guardsmen and ready to start their rigorous training. *"Most of the training was foot drill and rifle drill. Several afternoons were spent in the lecture hall, first of all learning the art of field craft, then on to more of the advanced training of use of the rifle and light infantry weapons"*.

The weekly Commanding Officer's Parade meant pressing uniform and much spit and polish. Any failure to look perfectly turned out also reflected on the trained guardsman in charge of them meaning their presentation was crucial to an easier path through training. *"Physical training instruction was held most days and in a few weeks, I felt fitter than I had ever felt in my life"*.

After six weeks of training, they were finally allowed to venture into the local town provided they passed the inspection of the trained guardsman and the sergeant of the guardroom. *"We spent our first evening out in a little pub in Guildford. Here the place was full of guardsmen from our barracks, most likely some of them enjoying their first night out like we were"*.

A further two months elapsed of intense training before a leave period was granted.

Note

1   Derrick Jackson's full account can be found *at www.britain-at-war.org. uk/WW2*

4

Home leave

On the 1st of September 1944 Basil and the rest of his intake were granted one week's Privilege Leave. Having passed the scrutiny of the Guardroom Sergeant, Basil would have arrived home looking as smart as any other Coldstream Guardsman. Despite her worries, Lillian was immensely proud of him. She marvelled at his perfectly 'bulled' boots and commented on mine when I first saw her after my initial training in the Police Force. Bulling boots is a skill that I never properly mastered as well as Basil would have done. It involves carefully laying shoe polish onto the toes of the boots and when dry, spitting onto a fine cloth and very carefully rubbing in small circles until the polish is so shiny you can literally see your reflection in it.

Basil stepped inside the back door. He was with one of his friends. They were both wearing peaked caps and Iris noted how polished their brass cap badges were and how smart they both looked, although predictably she thought Basil looked smarter. Basil was taller than his friend, who

I suspect was probably Fred or George. That evening Mary convinced them both to go with her and Sybil Hawkes to the dance at Marcham Village Hall. Mary loved dancing and went to all the local venues as often as she could, usually with her friend Sybil. They were reluctant to go but she wanted to show them off as they were far smarter than any of the other soldiers who went there from local bases. They relented and cycled the six miles to Marcham and back again on borrowed cycles. Basil's friend stayed the night after the dance, before presumably making his way onward to his own family.

Mary wasn't the only one who loved dancing. Hazel, for some time, had been cycling all the way to Didcot with her friends to the popular dances held there. Didcot was the location of a large logistics base, Foxhall Barracks, located next to the railway that had rapidly expanded during the lead up to D-Day and soldiers from there, together with airmen from nearby RAF Harwell were always at these dances. It was at one of these dances that she met Jim who was based at Foxhall Barracks. They had married in April prior to Basil 'joining up'. The Best Man was supposed to have been Jim's elder brother John MacHenry, but he was away undergoing intense training and denied leave for the wedding.

Life went on just as Basil had left it. The only main difference was that there was no man about the house. Their father, George, had passed away just before the outbreak of war with a chronic heart condition. Ken, the eldest, had moved away to Cornwall before the war had started, following building work as he was a brick layer. His recuperation from being shot in the knee was at a new address in Marston, Oxford with his wife Mary (Stevens). Curly was still away in the RAF. It was Basil then, who had dug the garden and planted and tended to the vegetables, who fed and cared for the chickens, who emptied the outdoor toilet bucket every day and dug the contents into the garden. It was Basil who had done the day-to-day little maintenance jobs and made a significant contribution to the household finances.

He must have been dismayed to see the garden in such a state with weeds growing amongst the fully grown vegetables. He would have spent many hours throughout March, April, and May, until his join-up date in June, preparing the soil and planting them with great care. At just eighteen he was a very experienced gardener. He had tended the school garden together with two or three other boys in the school rather than attend some of the lessons. This seems to have been allowed at that time, probably due to the fact that the school garden produced vegetables that were in great demand due to the rationing that had been in force since the start of the war. He would have left instructions on when and how much to water, and when to pick them. In his quieter moments I am sure he would have thought about them, wondering how they had grown, how the family would be enjoying them on a Sunday, with sausages, or rabbit, or maybe a fat cockerel.

The fact was that everyone at home had their hands full with hard work. Iris and Vera were too young to be tasked with gardening jobs and were still at school. Mary worked in the cigarette booth at the nearby munitions factory hidden in Tubney Woods where they manufactured bombs and artillery shells. Working in the booth was said to be the start of her lifelong smoking habit. The old munitions factory no longer exists as it has now been rebuilt as a new factory. Hazel worked long night shifts at the Morris factory making aircraft parts so slept until late afternoon.

The hardest working of all was Lillian, who was up early every morning to clean, 'black', and light the coal fired range. She was used to hard work. She had started in 'service' as a scullery maid in a large house in London from an early age and had worked in several similar such houses until she married George, in 1916 during his leave from serving in the Royal Veterinary Corps. in the First World War. George, a local lad from the village, left the Veterinary Corps. to become a builder. He was a keen cricketer and supporter of the Cumnor Cricket Club, usually acting as Umpire during matches. Between them they had seven children, so her life was always one of intense hard work, especially so after he passed away. She cleaned Mrs Walker's house just around Moss's Corner, and Mrs Blackwell's house, next to the village pond. Her family-owned Blackwell's Book Shop in Broad St Oxford. She also cleaned Fred Baker's shop in the village at 6pm after closing time, it was a wooden hut then. She washed the vicar's surplices (gowns) and starched and ironed them. She also took in other people's washing which she washed outside in the wash house using two or three tin baths. These would have doubled as baths for everyone in the house when placed in front of the fire in the kitchen. I even recall being bathed as a young child in one. The house had an outside toilet with a bucket under a scrubbed pine bench, which was still the only toilet until I was around six years old. Lillian took over emptying the bucket every day when Basil left.

Mary collected and delivered the laundry. Iris often went with her as she occasionally got a penny tip. On one occasion, Mary lost the half a crown payment in the Closes fields and they both had to go back and find it, which luckily, they did.

Half a crown was quite a lot of money back then. Hazel and Mary paid their mother some keep which helped out.

It must have been even harder for Lillian seeing him off at the end of his short leave, as when he joined up back in June. The war had been raging in Normandy and the BBC Radio News and the newspapers were full of the advances being made, but also of the losses.

Return from leave would have seen a move to the next level of Coldstream Guards training, this time at Pirbright camp near Farnborough, Hampshire.

There they were to find the conditions much the same as at Caterham although training was much more strenuous, but far more interesting as they began handling infantry weapons on the ranges. There was also training on the throwing of the hand grenades. Other days were filled with route marches, sometimes at night, and orienteering style events requiring map reading and time management. These were seen as the hardest of all, having to run many exhausting miles as a group over difficult terrain, working up a sweat and then chilling in the cold October nights. As Derrick Jackson put it – *"Our training was severe, but I enjoyed every minute of it and began to feel real fit."*.

5

An aerial spectacle

Back in Cumnor, Mr and Mrs Money lived in the other half of the red brick, semi-detached house with their daughters – Sisley, Cynthia, and Kath, and son Dan (Basil's friend). Iris was friends with them all and has remained friends with them all her life. At the time of writing Iris at 92 years and Sisley at 96 years telephone each other regularly. Mr and Mrs Webb lived next door on the other side with daughter Sheila. Next to them were Mr and Mrs Trinder with their four children. All four houses had, and still have a magnificent view from the upstairs front windows. Looking out of the window to the left, it is possible to see as far as Faringdon Folly and White Horse Hill. In the foreground, about one mile away, the farm buildings of Farrant's Farm can be seen. The red double decker service bus was visible whilst still more than a mile from the house, allowing a two minute warning to whoever was to catch it, making them rush around to get to the bus stop across the road in time. Across the road is a thick hedge partially masking a large field belonging to Farrant's Farm. Beyond that the land sweeps gently down towards the river Thames, but is masked by a ridge in Farrant's field. Across the river the land gently rises into the distance where on a clear day Brize Norton, about 12 miles away can be clearly seen. 10 miles beyond Brize Norton is Fairford in Gloucestershire. During the war the Gloucestershire airfields of Broadwell, Fairford, Down Ampney and Blakehill Farm were active bases specialising in glider towing.

On Sunday morning, 17th September 1944, Iris, Lillian, and Vera ran outside as large planes towing gliders roared over the house at rooftop height, struggling to gain altitude with engines at full throttle. The house shook and the noise was deafening. All the neighbours, including their respective evacuees, were out staring at the sky through a low mist that had formed up to the height of the rooftops. They were seeing five Squadrons of C47 Dakotas taking off from these bases, towing dozens of Horsa Gliders. All were laden with troops of the 1st Airborne Division and other supporting airborne units as part of Operation Market Garden. Having taken off from separate airfields, they all converged roughly over the house before setting course for Nijmegen and Arnhem in Holland. This aerial spectacle lasted over an hour. Vera stood outside the house gazing up as plane after plane passed over. The overwhelming noise of the aircraft, and the faces of the crews looking down at them captivating her. She noticed that Lillian was crying. Could it have been because of the worry that one might crash onto the house? Or was it that seeing the aircraft obviously on route to a large-scale attack reminded her that Basil would soon be in mortal danger wherever they were heading? Or did she think that perhaps Basil may have been in one of those gliders? Any of these would have set her anxiety racing.

News soon spread around the village that one of the gliders had crashed into the trees off the Besselsleigh Road having struck electrical high-tension wires, decapitating the pilot. People cycled to the scene which was less than a mile away. The paratroopers in the glider thought that they had landed in enemy territory as they had been flying for some time trying to gain height. As a consequence, they started to 'round up' the locals at gun point as they approached the crash site until they were convinced that they were still in England.[1]

The following day the second 'lift' took place. This time with more favourable weather over England the gliders and tugs flew higher and were not directly over the house as before. None of them knew it at the time but Jim's brother John MacHenry was in the back of one of those gliders with his team of gunners from the 2nd Airlanding Anti-tank Battery, Royal Artillery, together with their 6 – pounder artillery gun and jeep lashed to the wooden floor of the Horsa Glider. The Germans had been taken by surprise the day before and thus the gliders landed mostly unopposed with only the skill of the pilots and luck to ensure a safe landing. It was a vastly different story for the second 'lift'. German forces had been steadily pouring into the area and the landing zones were in grave danger of being overrun. Many gliders landed under considerable ground fire, the pilots and passengers having to conduct the tricky job of removing the rear ends of the gliders to extricate their loads whilst under enemy machine gun fire. John MacHenry was the Lance Sergeant in charge of one of the 6 pounder artillery guns and its crew. After struggling to get the gun out of the Horsa he and the crew were in immediate action laying fire on the enemy positions around the perimeter of their landing zone. He was shot in the stomach during this action. He and the six other men and an officer from his battery wounded in this action were taken to the nearby makeshift casualty station.[2]

Notes

1   The Glider was a Horsa HS101, (chalk mark 240) the pilot was Sgt 3653210 Thomas Anthony Joyce, aged 25, a Liverpudlian in E Squadron, 11 Flt, 1st Wing. The co-pilot was Sgt Hoyle who was seriously injured but survived. Sgt Joyce was the first fatality of the operation that day. He is buried in West Derby Cemetery, Liverpool, with his mother and father.

2   Lance Serjeant 404421 John MacHenry died on the 22nd of September 1944 of his wound, aged 30 years old, 5 days into the fated mission. He is buried at Oosterbeek War Cemetery, Arnhem, Netherlands. His headstone is engraved – '*And you shall wave at the stars that all is well*'

6

Embarkation leave

On 11th November 1944 Basil and 'the boys' as I will now refer to them as, all received 'change of station leave' for two weeks. This is also known as 'embarkation leave' prior to going overseas. Their families would have noticed a significant change in them. Their athletic physique with smaller waist and muscular limbs, their stance, their confidence, their attitude, all changed. 'Their haircuts so sharp you could cut yourself on them'. These were men trained to fight. Competent in bayonetting Germans disguised as sandbags on ropes. Able to simulate mortal combat with and without weapons on each other. Able to attack sand bagged positions as a cohesive unit and much more. Big fish in a very small pond.

As per his last leave, Floss would have been there to greet him as enthusiastically as ever. Floss was Basil's dog. A Golden Retriever that he had lavished huge amounts of his time on to train and nurture into the obedient, loyal, good natured friend she had become. Lillian, Iris, Hazel, Mary and Vera would have all rushed to the door to greet him and would have marvelled at how fit and strong he looked. Lillian would have taken his kit bag off him and put his clothes out for washing. She would have fed him and done her best to take care of his every need. He would have checked out the garden, chatted to Dan next door and spent a lot of time on the chair in front of the fire in the kitchen. At some point he would have almost certainly visited Farrant's farm on this leave. The farm would have been much as he had left it, only he had changed. It must have been a memorable experience for Mr Farrant and Jack Miller to see the farm boy they knew as Basil turning up looking immaculate with his bulled boots, pressed uniform and a new aura of confidence.

Lillian will have fussed over him the whole time he was at home, feeding him up, and listening to his stories about the training. He would only ever have given her the good bits. He would have told her all about the antics of Mansel, George, Paul and Fred, about their families, their previous jobs, and their lives. Lillian would have known that his return would mean going to the war in Europe. Basil himself wouldn't have known where exactly he was going but both would have known that he was soon to go into a dangerous world. Since the D-Day landings in June the casualty listings had been fearsome. It's hard to imagine how Lillian dealt with this. Her youngest son was potentially never coming back. Hard work and too many woodbine cigarettes would have been how she coped.

7

Belgium

This would be the last time Basil and the boys saw home for a further nine months. That leave signified the end of training and the new posting to their battalion. They were all allocated to the 5th Battalion of the Coldstream Guards who were already in Belgium. The battalion had arrived in Normandy on 23rd June to an area west of Bayeux ready to take part in Operation Goodwood, the attack that would force the Germans back from Caen and finally establish a secure foothold in France. They were involved in heavy fighting where the Germans were surrounded at Falaise in Normandy. They fought their way across France and into Belgium, liberating Brussels on the 3rd of September. They were again involved in heavy fighting east of Brussels near Bourg Leopold and the advance into Holland as part of Operation Market Garden (as per the film 'A Bridge Too Far'). The battalion were then allowed to retire to winter quarters on the 21st of December at the small, undamaged by war village of Opheylissem, east of Brussels.

The boys will have heard whilst in training of how well the 'Fighting Fifths,' as they were popularly known as, were doing in France, Belgium and Holland. They will have heard of heroic acts such as Major Hill's Distinguished Service Order awarded for his actions at Bourg Leopold. There were plenty of other acts of bravery from all ranks. What the boys in training would not have been told was that the battalion had suffered catastrophic casualties. 3 Company ceased to exist after Bourg Leopold. The Officers were all dead or wounded. Many of the men in that company were killed or wounded. The rest of the Battalion wasn't in much better shape. Including officers, a total of 147 of the 5th Battalion had been killed and many times more wounded. The desperately needed stay in Opheylissem enabled the battalion to re-equip, reinforce with new recruits, and to enable some to have desperately needed leave passes home.

The 5th Battalion was an Infantry (foot) battalion, made up of a Battalion Headquarters, a Support Company, and four forward (Rifle) Companies numbered 1 to 4.[1] It is difficult to establish exact numbers, but the battalion would have had approximately 850 men. Each company would have approximately 100 – 150 men. Wherever possible I will refer to the 5th Battalion as simply 'the battalion' from now on.

From the 1st of January 1945, in overall command of the battalion was Lieutenant-Colonel E.R. Hill DSO. Basil, Mansel, George, Fred and Paul were assigned to '4 Company' commanded by Major J.d'H. Hamilton, the third company commander in the six months since D-Day. Second in command was Captain Ian Liddell who transferred from Headquarters staff into 4 Company shortly before the boys arrived. Lieutenant Michael Wall was the only survivor of the company's three Platoon Commanders from D Day and was thus by far the most battle experienced officer.

It was to Major Hamilton then that the boys were ordered to report to, but first they had to face what would have been a tense and uncomfortable sailing in a troop ship to Ostend in Belgium. They would have been issued with three sick bags for the journey, a 24 hour ration pack and an emergency supply of chocolate in a tin which could only be opened with permission from an officer. The weather was perishingly cold with snow falling over much of northern Europe. They arrived to find many buildings had been completely destroyed, or badly damaged. The destruction had happened in two main waves. At the beginning of the war it was bombed by British bombers rendering many of the buildings into empty shells. After the D-Day landings, the Germans blew up much of the port infrastructure that would have been vital in re-enforcing the allied armies. Luckily not all the port facilities were destroyed, and it was usable whilst the recently captured larger port of Antwerp was being cleared ready for use. It continued to be used for troop movements, even after Antwerp was opened up to shipping at the end of November thus freeing up Antwerp to be mainly used for supplies. In any event Ostend would have been a hive of activity for the allies with baggage laden soldiers from all units arriving. Some lucky soldiers would have been going home on leave, and more of the not so lucky, on stretchers. The sight of the returning wounded must have been an unnerving shock to Basil and the boys.

The capture of Antwerp, and later the estuary, referred to now as the Battle Of the River Scheldt, was vital to the allied advance across Europe as all the supplies, including fuel for the tanks and lorries had to come via the temporary Mulberry

Harbour at Normandy and be transported by road to the front line that had by the end of 1944 reached the German border. Antwerp is very close to the German border and was the largest and most useful to the Allies. The Germans had made a very successful job of denying all the Channel Ports to the allies by extensive demolition and sabotage. The Canadians had led the task of capturing them. Antwerp was finally captured and both banks of the River Scheldt cleared of Germans by the 8th of November at terrifying cost to the Canadians, Polish and British troops involved. The Germans wanted it back. In December they had launched a full-scale attack through the Ardennes region into Belgium and headed north towards Antwerp. It became known famously as 'The Battle of the Bulge'. The attack had fallen on the American sector and with colossal loss they held onto the town of Bastogne. By the end of the year, once the skies cleared, the German armoured columns were attacked by fighter bombers which slowed them considerably but their advance continued.

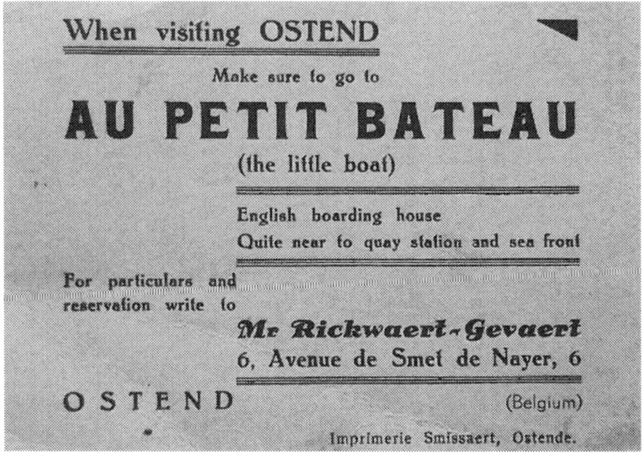

Business card relating to Au Petit Bateau in Ostend, Belgium

I found a business card in the envelope of documents and photographs. It pertains to a Guest House in Ostend called 'Au Petit Bateau' at 6 Avenue de Smet de Nayer. On the rear is written and underlined in pencil 'Jan 6th 1945'. This business card is the first piece of hard evidence I have that Basil arrived in Europe. 6 Avenue de Smet de Nayer exists to this day albeit having been rebuilt during a modernisation of the entire street in the 1990s. It is impossible to determine if Basil actually stayed there or merely that he saw the business card and kept it as a souvenir of the fact that he had been in Ostend on that date. The weather was so atrocious that the recruits would have certainly been housed with host families or boarding houses thus his stay there is highly likely and may well have been for a few days. A lorry sent from Bourg Leopold (renamed Leopoldsburg today) to collect them went missing for a few days, prompting an officer being assigned to enquire as to its whereabouts before turning up there, its delay being due to the treacherous road conditions.

Their route would have taken them via battle-scarred Antwerp before arriving at the reinforcement's facility within the vast military complex that was Bourg Leopold. Thanks to the 5th Battalion's earlier capture of it, it had quickly become a huge storage and transit camp for munitions, supplies, and reinforcements to all the various units in the area. It was based at what was and still is the Belgium army's main barracks. From there they would have been transported to the battalion's winter rest site at Opheylissem.

Arrival at Opheylissem must have come as a huge surprise to the boys. They had experienced six months of harsh intense training, been subjected to every abuse, had journeyed through the still unsafe mine infested waters of the

English Channel and travelled in uncomfortable open trucks across war torn areas of Belgium. To the rest of the battalion, the battle hardened survivors of the advance through France, Opheylissem must have seemed like paradise compared to the slaughter and depravation they had suffered. Under such circumstances, if J.R.R. Tolkien had only been in the 5th Battalion, this place could have been his inspiration for his mystical *Rivendell*. The village was a winter wonderland. The houses lay on a gentle slope and were covered in layers of deep snow falls. At the bottom of the slope was a typically Gallic chateau looking magnificent in its coating of snow. Food was plentiful and relations with villagers with whom they shared their homes with was cordial, so cordial that before the end of their stay there were several marriages. At the beginning of January, the battalion officers held a huge dinner party at the chateau, inviting officers from all around the area. The candlelit banquet of dozens of turkeys was washed down with 81 bottles of champagne, one per officer. The Regimental Band provided the entertainment. While the officers were so engaged, I'm sure the men would have had their own beer, feast, and fun, albeit there is no record of it. The Regimental Band stayed until the 10th of January and provided concerts for all the men, in the evenings there were company dances and cinema shows. In this idyllic backwater, apart from frequent high altitude bomber formations passing overhead, and V1 Flying Bombs passing the other way, the war must have seemed a long way off.

There was just one problem. Opheylissem was right in the path of the German advance on Antwerp, and it is a well documented fact that the Germans used some of their troops to cause confusion and sabotage behind the Allied lines by dressing as allied military police. The companies had therefore to patrol the roads around the area, some of which were impassable due to the snow, with the aim of looking out for these 'spies'. As recent arrivals it is likely that the boys were engaged in this activity as part of their 'hardening up'. No 'spies' were found and the offensive had petered out by late January.

In amongst the patrols all the companies had two drill parades per week and a route march to get them in shape for whatever the future was to hold for them. No one seemed to mind this as they were able to return to their warm billets in the evenings. Basil and the boys' time at Opheylissem must have felt like a strange adventure, doing exactly what they already knew in training but in a far more relaxed atmosphere. Amid the battle hardened survivors though, they must have felt considerably smaller fish in a much larger pond. They had it all to prove.

Whilst still at Opheylissem, on the 25th of January, Basil was authorised 72 hours 'Privilege Leave'. It wouldn't have been possible in the time available to visit home. The alternative would have been to perhaps visit Brussels, which was definitely a popular attraction with life feeling almost like peacetime after its liberation. In fact, he may well have already visited Brussels prior to the privilege leave as life at Opheylissem was quite relaxed and day trips were common, being only an hour away. Brussels had a special draw to the battalion as it were they who were first to liberate the town.

On his return, he started a course of typhus vaccinations. Around this time there were ominous reports of typhus epidemics in some of the bombed out towns in Germany and in the concentration camps that were by now known about, but not the magnitude of the problem. It is likely that the whole battalion were vaccinated at the same time as Basil.

On 31st January the Corps Commander arrived to brief the battalion on its next mission. Basil, Mansel, George, Fred and Paul's refuge from harm's way was at an end. To use the Tolkien analogy again, the boys were soon to pass through the 'gates of *Mordor*'.

Note

1   Basil's 5th Battalion Coldstream formed part of the infantry element of the '32nd *Guards Brigade*', which also included Irish Guards, and Welsh Guards in Churchill Tanks, 'Royal Artillery', Royal Engineers, and other specialist units. They, together with the '5th *Guards Armoured Brigade*' (Grenadier Guards, 1st Battalion Coldstream in Sherman Tanks, Irish Guards, 'Royal Artillery', Royal Engineers, and other specialist units) formed a 'self contained' fighting force, named the '*Guards Armoured Division*' (800 vehicles and 3,000 men).

Experience of the fighting in western Europe identified that very close co-operation between infantry and tanks was a necessity for fighting effectiveness, therefore on the 23rd of February 1945 Basil's 5th Battalion Coldstream were attached to the '5th *Guards Armoured Brigade*' . Within the Brigade they were teamed with the 1st Battalion Coldstream Tanks such that each of the four 5th Battalion Coldstream infantry (rifle) companies were paired with their respective 1st Battalion Coldstream Squadrons (Called squadrons rather than companies as they were in tanks). They were then referred to as '*The Coldstream Group*'. This pairing proved effective and was used extensively until the end of the war.

At certain periods the 5th Battalion were temporarily loaned to other Divisions.

The '*Guards Armoured Division*' came under the command of '*XXX Corps*' until 17th April 1945, when it was moved to '*XII Corps*'.

XXX Corps, XII Corps, VIII Corps, and I Corps collectively formed the 2nd British Army, which together with the 1st Canadian Army formed the 21st Army Group.

The references to these Armies, Corps, Divisions, and Brigades creates confused reading unless fully familiar with army structures. Therefore unless deemed necessary, such as the battle for Haus Loo in Chapter 17, I have focussed in on what Basil and the boys of 4 Company actually experienced, therefore it should be assumed that in many actions they were involved in, they were part of a bigger picture. A breakdown of these structures can be found in Addendum VI.

8

Operation Veritable

The briefing was for Operation Veritable, later to be referred to as the Battle for the Rhineland. It is useful at this point to have an overview of Operation Veritable and the situation that the allies found themselves in at the beginning of 1945 as it was to be this bloody crucible that Basil and the boys were to be thrown into.

In the latter half of 1944 supplies of fuel and munitions being transported from Normandy could not keep up with the rapid allied advance and thus shortages of fuel prevented a full scale 'broad front' assault on the German border. Field Marshal Montgomery, in charge of the entire British and Canadian 21st Army Group, successfully argued the case to attempt to force a 'narrow front' over the Rhine and into Germany via the intact bridge at Arnhem and end the war early without waiting for the channel ports to be liberated and brought back into action. This was a dramatic failure and thus plans were made to conduct a 'broad front' advance on Germany and cross the Rhine river at multiple points north and south of Cologne. These plans were hampered until the port of Antwerp was opened up and made usable for supplies to sustain such a huge advance. The totally unexpected German counterattack we now call the Battle of the Bulge then further delayed the plans. Additionally, the American failure to capture the Roer Dams that dominated the Rhineland frustrated Field Marshal Montgomery's plan to attack there. Montgomery's plan involved the American 9th Army in the south and the British/Canadian 21st Army in the north attacking across the German border in a 'pincer' movement and capturing the part of Germany between its western border and the river Rhine. In doing so, to destroy or capture the German forces located there so that when the eventual crossing of the Rhine took place, they would have less resistance. The Americans were to cross the river Roer and head northeast. The British and Canadians were to attack from Nijmegen in Holland and head southeast between the River Maas and the River Rhine to meet the Americans near Wesel, thus clearing the west bank of the Rhine of German forces. The American part of the attack was called Operation Grenade and the British/Canadian attack called Operation Veritable. For political reasons Operation Veritable was to be Canadian led albeit there were far more British troops involved.

It was hoped that the attack would have taken place in mid winter to take advantage of the hard frozen ground. The unavoidable delays meant that the snow was melting and the ground turning to mud. In addition to this the Germans had been very busy building their defences. They had destroyed sluices and dams that very effectively caused the Rhine and other rivers to flood a huge area, isolating villages and submerging roads. The Americans found themselves completely halted on the banks of the river Roer due to the Germans destroying dams upstream that turned the river into an impassable torrent of flood water. The Germans were masters of 'defence in depth' during the First World War and drew on this knowledge when arranging the border defences they called their 'Western Wall'. We called it the 'Siegfried Line'. It consisted of trench lines, anti-tank ditches, land mines, concrete machine gun emplacements, barbed wire, concrete dugouts, and fortified farms all strategically placed to create the best possible killing fields and in some places to a depth of over a mile.

The British/Canadian sector in front of Nijmegen was dominated by the dense Reichswald Forest right in the centre line of the attack on the German border. There are just two roads out of Nijmegen into Germany. The one to the north of the forest, heads east towards the medieval town of Kleve (most famous as the home of Henry the Eighth's wife Anne of Cleaves). The other road passes to the south of the forest and heads south towards Gennep in Holland, then east towards the town of Goch in Germany. East of Kleve and Goch is the river Rhine. The plan for Operation Veritable was to first capture Kleve and the high ground around it. Then to head south and capture Goch, whilst clearing the Reichswald Forest and area between Kleve and Goch. Once secured, the Guards Armoured Division (held in reserve and which Basil was part of) would break through and capture the Rhine bridges at Wesel and meet up with the Americans attacking from the south. It was planned to take just four days to reach Wesel but that was far from what actually happened.

The build up started three weeks before the attack and

was to take place in the strictest of secrecy, with movements only taking place at night. 340,000 people including front line troops were involved in the preparation. 10,000 tons of equipment were transported every night, meaning that the poor quality roads had to be repaired and re-repaired. Over 1,200 aircraft, mostly bombers and ground attack Typhoons, and 1000 artillery and other types of guns were readied. 500 tanks, with a further 500 in reserve were moved up to the start line. There were also 500 'funnies'. These were various types of armoured vehicles of special design. The 'Buffalo' was a tracked vehicle capable of carrying 24 men or equipment through water and muddy conditions. Primarily intended for amphibious landings but perfectly suited to dealing with flooded areas as they had special tracks that acted as paddles to propel them. The 'Weasel' was similar in purpose to the Buffalo but much smaller and able to be carried within Buffalos. The 'Kangaroo' (I'm not making this up) was a Sherman Tank with the turret removed to act as a personnel carrier. 'Crocodiles' were Churchill tanks equipped with flamethrowers. Smaller Bren carriers equipped with flamethrowers were called 'Wasps'. There were also special tanks with revolving chains (Flails) in front of them used to clear mines by exploding them as the chains hit them. These were known as 'Crabs'. Others carried fascines, (bundles of wood) to fill in antitank ditches, or bobbins, which were wound coil and tubular scaffolding carpets for laying a track over mud for wheeled vehicles. Finally there were Terrapins, the British version of the American 'DUKW', which was a large amphibious, wheeled vehicle for carrying men and supplies across water

The 75,000 assault troops to be involved in Operation

Veritable had been congregating for weeks and spread over a wide area just south of Antwerp. It was no coincidence then that Basil and the battalion had been sent to Opheylissem to get back to fighting strength.

The attack was set for the 8th of February 1945. Five nights beforehand, all the troops involved in the initial attack had moved to their assembly areas around Nijmegen. There followed the biggest artillery bombardment yet seen in the European campaign lasting 5½ hours, after which the attack started. The Germans were not expecting this to be the main attack and had only placed 10,000 poorly trained elderly men and boys in the Reichswald Forest and Kleve area. Further south in the Goch area they had 2,000 of the well equipped, highly trained, and motivated Parachutists. Not surprisingly the attack went well at first. By day three, despite a blunder that caused the biggest military traffic jam of the war, the high ground around Kleve had been captured via the north road and the Canadians had cleared the flooded area between the north road and the Rhine. The Reichswald forest was slowly being cleared and Gennep was captured via the southerly road. However, Goch had not been captured and the attack was slowing down. The enemy at this point was not only the Germans, it was the floods and the mud, creating conditions similar to those experienced during the Battle of Passchendaele in the First World War. The flooded waters of the Rhine were rising and parts of the Nijmegen to Kleve Road were under four feet of water. Elsewhere the tanks were finding movement all but impossible. The Germans finally recognised that this was the main attack and in the knowledge that the Americans were still unable to cross the flooded river Roer they had moved some of their elite forces to the north to meet the threat. Hitler had given his predictable order that he gave to all his forces who were in danger of giving ground – No Surrender, fight to the last man! The scene was set for one of the bloodiest set piece battles of World War 2. Enter our boys, eventually.

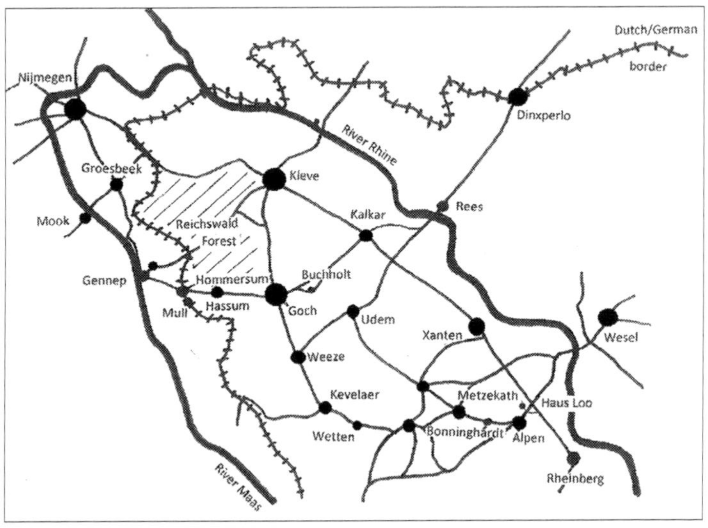

Map of area fought over in Operation Veritable

9

Preparing for battle

Basil and the battalion were to be held in reserve to wait their turn to deploy. Only on the 5th of February had all the officers in the battalion been briefed on Operation Veritable and not until the 7th did they leave for their new holding position at Haaren, southwest of Nijmegen in Holland. This proved to be a nightmare journey in trucks and assorted vehicles, 14 hours were spent on the road due to diversions, collapse of roads in places, and floods. One vehicle had an accident and the driver was killed. That night they would have been awakened by the sound of 1,000 heavy bombers pulverising Kleve, and other towns in the way of the advance, reducing them to rubble. At 5.00am they would have been awakened by the distant loud apocalyptic roar of 1,000 heavy guns bursting into life. To the west of them the night was lit by a full spectrum of incandescent flashes.

It must have been a frustrating and unnerving time for Basil, the boys, and the whole battalion for that matter, stuck at Haaren awaiting orders to move forward that were made and cancelled several times. This was unfortunately to be the pattern over the next few days. In my time in the police we used to call this depressingly common event 'hurry up and wait'. There is always a plus side, the boys got hot meals and warm beds courtesy of local Belgians rather than being stuck on open roads in uncomfortable trucks eating cold rations.

Finally in the late morning of the 11th of February Basil and the battalion headed towards their new forward position at Groesbeek, a few miles southeast of Nijmegen. Basil must have experienced feelings of elation, mixed with trepidation at being part of such a gigantic build-up of troops and supplies. The sounds of battle would have been heard from Haaren but as they grew nearer it would have been becoming all too real with the sound of hellish gunfire ever more present. It was to be of course the first time that he or the boys were heading to the 'front'. Their 'holiday like' experiences of Belgium were over, and a new sinister chapter was building up before them.

It was to prove once again to be a nightmare journey. In the afternoon they arrived at Malden, to the south of Nijmegen after a detour made necessary by the state of the roads; the original route being impassable. Here it was found that the battalion area had been changed from Groesbeek, to the southeast part of Nijmegen town. This being owed to the very dilapidated state of Groesbeek. The column turned about and despite constant rain, the state of the roads and interminable traffic congestion slowing things up they finally arrived at their allotted billets in Nijmegen by late evening. The billets were very close to heavy guns so that every time they fired a shell it made everyone jump out of their skin.

The next day at 10am they were put on four hours' notice to move off, and then again at 6pm with six hours' notice.

They didn't move out from their warm billets in the end until the afternoon of the 13th of February and then it was forward into Groesbeek again. The battalion had fought here in late 1944, before Basil joined them, when it had been heavily shelled and the buildings had all the roof tiles blown off. It was raining hard so the whole battalion set about retiling the roofs and consequently were able to have some respite from the cold and very wet weather. As did many in the battalion, Basil and boys could walk through the wrecked trenches and barbed wire of the old battlefield and climb a low hill, the highest in Holland. From there they could see across the flat land devastated by the attack to the ominous Reichswald Forest and the vast flooded region to the north. They would have been able to see gun positions steadily firing towards the front and feel their percussion on their chests. The boys knew they would be going that way very soon. One can only wonder at what their thoughts were.

Whilst they were relocating into Groesbeek, Gennep had been captured. It was an important supply route for the British troops as the northern route was becoming increasingly impassable due to the floods. By now the battle hardened German Parachute Regiments, skilled in close combat and executing last-ditch stands, and elite Panzer (tank) divisions had arrived outside Kleve, Gennep, Goch and the Reichswald Forest to dramatically strengthen the defence by more than three times their number. The fighting from now on would take on a far more bitter character.

The ground conditions across the whole battlefield had made use of tanks almost impossible and thus the Guards Armoured Division remained in reserve. However, their 32nd Guards Brigade, containing Basil and the battalion were infantry. Consequently, on the 13th of February they were temporarily transferred to the command of the 51st Highland Division who had fought their way through the Reichswald Forest and captured Gennep.

East of Gennep was to be the area the battalion were to attack the next day, as part of the grinding advance towards the town of Goch from the west. Meanwhile other British forces were attacking towards Goch from the north.

Life goes on at home

The mysterious RAF Camp[1] set up down the road had proved irresistible to the local youths; including Iris, Cynthia, the Trinders, and their respective evacuees. It wasn't long before they crept into the khaki green marquee. The men were very friendly and with little else to do they spent hours on most days in the marquee. Inside, the furnishing was sparse with six beds in one corner and desks and chairs in the remainder. On one particular occasion one of the men exclaimed "The officer is outside! What are we going to do with you lot? Quick get under the beds." They all dutifully dived under the beds and hid silently whilst the officer talked to the men. When he had gone they crept out but the experience frightened Iris and she went home.

It wasn't long before the RAF men were familiar with the adults in the road and two in particular frequented the house where they sat in the kitchen chatting. One showed a particular interest in Mary. She reciprocated and dated him a few times before the older one turned up alone one day. He explained that he thought his friend to be unsuitable for Mary as he already had a girl he was engaged to back home. This ended Mary's interest in him but the revelation led to the older one, Les, becoming a family friend who then came alone regularly. He was a jovial man with an excellent singing voice and skills on the piano. He never got to play the old piano in the kitchen as it was way out of tune but he did frequent The Bear and Ragged Staff up the road and often played the piano and led the singing in the bulging pub full of Les's RAF friends, locals, and Americans from the Besselsleigh Camp. Due to their presence at The Bear and Ragged Staff their camp was soon known to all in the village and there were many visits from local girls and some courting went on.

The week before Christmas, Les and the other men pulled out a surprise. They invited everyone they had met in the village to a Christmas dance in the marquee. A band played and everyone crammed inside, with many more outside dancing and drinking. It was a memorable and heart lifting occasion.

A wartime Christmas was most likely a quiet and low key affair. A cockerel would have been Christmas dinner at the house. Entertainment was really only provided by an old square wooden-sided valve radio placed on a chair in the kitchen. The piano in the kitchen was only there to be used as an item of furniture as they had little else other than wooden chairs. Lillian's sister owned a pub in Wendlebury, and when the pub's piano was worn she would hand it to her other sister, who in turn would hand down her piano to Lillian. Basil's dog, Floss, slept under the piano. When George was alive, he insisted on listening to the six o'clock news from the BBC, on pain of early bed if anyone dared to interrupt it. Listening to the news at six thus became the norm but throughout the war most households listened in.

Apart from daily news of the progress with the RAF Bomber Command air campaign there was little else in the way of uplifting news. The amazing news of the advances after D-Day had fallen flat. The failure of the attempt to enter Germany via Holland at Arnhem, followed by the German attack we now know as the 'Battle of the Bulge' provided the most depressing news. It would have seemed like the war was to go on a lot longer.

On Christmas day though, there was more gloomy news when the BBC announced that Glenn Miller was missing. He was the legendary big band leader whose music cheered the war-weary and thrilled a generation. He had vanished on Christmas Eve over the English Channel while flying from Britain to France.

New Year came and went. They were now into the sixth year of the war. The news was still about speculation of Glenn Miller's fate and slightly more optimistic news that the German attack had been slowed. Disney animated films had been very popular throughout the war and news of the first new production for over two years must have come as a welcome treat. 'The Three Caballeros', starring Donald Duck had been released in America and would be out soon in the local cinemas.

It wasn't just Basil over in Belgium that was experiencing the snow. January 1945 in England proved to be very cold. The temperature plummeted and snow was deep in parts of the country. A miserable time for all but the cold weather meant that the village pond iced over. The ice was so thick that it supported even the heaviest of adults. Great fun was had by all the village with people able to slide the full length of the pond.

On Friday the 9th of February 1945, they would have heard the BBC Radio News announce that an 11 hour artillery barrage and strong air support had launched British and Canadian troops on an assault into Germany on a five mile front between the River Maas and the Rhine.

Mercifully Lillian had no way of knowing that Basil was to be involved. Or that he was soon to be on his way to Nijmegen in preparation to join the attack. It was big news but so was the rationing and the V2 Rockets being dropped around London and the south east. The next day the BBC announced that the attack had widened to six miles and had advanced into Germany itself, breaking into the first Siegfried defence line.

The Siegfried Line was known by everyone at home due to the popular song – *'We're hanging out the washing on the Siegfried Line'*. They had little idea what it actually was or that within a few days Basil was to be in action for the first time and would be holding onto the Siegfried Line defences in the most appalling nightmarish conditions.

Note

1   The RAF Camp was set up less than 100 yards from the last house in the road. That house belonged to Mr Edmunds a senior Meteorological Office weather consultant who made a significant contribution to the decision to launch the D-Day landings. Although there is no concrete information, I suspect that the RAF Camp was a weather station associated with Mr Edmunds.

II

The first attack

The object of the battalion's attack was to expand the foothold gained across the river Niers at Gennep as part of the advance towards Goch by the 51st Highland Division. The river was in heavy flood, so any crossing point was at a premium and well worth consolidating by pushing forward at that point. On the morning of the 14th February the sun was shining with clear skies as Major J.d'H. Hamilton (the Battalion Commander) viewed the planned line of the attack from his elevated position in the church tower of the Dutch village of Ottersum.

The plan was for the Welsh Guards to attack eastwards out of Gennep and clear the large woodland, whilst Basil and the battalion would attack on their left through heather-covered sand dunes. Once at their objective two miles away, the Irish Guards would then pass through them and capture the German border village of Hommersum.

4 Company (Basil and the boys) would lead the attack, with 2 Company on their right. 4 Company's objective was the

area around a distinctive question mark shaped lake named *'Zeven Morgeziep'*, between Gennep and Hommersum, just south of *Heuvelenweg*. 1 and 3 Companies were to be held in reserve. The map attached to the war diary illustrates their final positions:

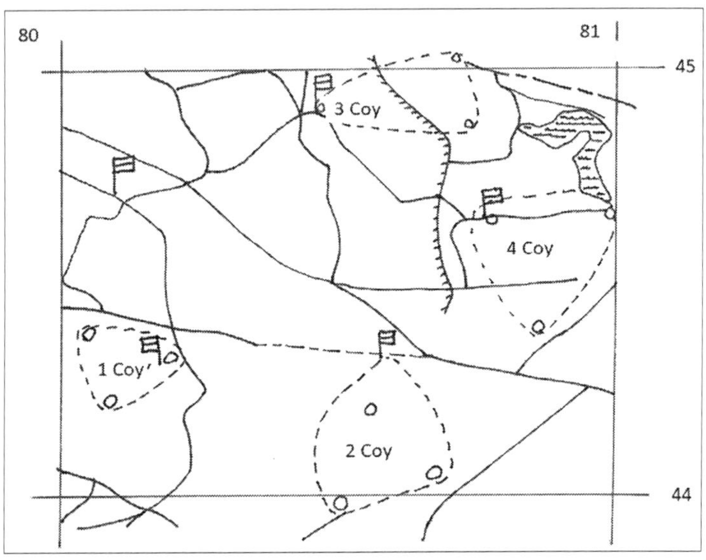

Battalion positions 14th February south-east of Gennep

Whilst Major J.d'H. Hamilton was still at Ottersum the battalion was being driven in Troop Carrying Lorries (TCLs) from Mook along *Rijksweg* and *Nijmeegseweg* where they debussed and marched over the only bridge over the river Niers, to a meeting point in the western half of Gennep itself. There they waited until 1pm when they marched across the small town to the start line behind the scrub covered dunes along *Stiemenseg* near its junction with *Randweg*. Again, they waited.

Suddenly there was a burst of machine gun fire from behind. One of the Welsh Guards' tanks in support of the attack had accidently fired its machine gun. The shocking result was one guardsman killed and several injured. Very alarming for everyone there waiting nervously for the attack to happen. At 2.00pm the information came back that the Germans had vacated the area to be attacked. The attack went in anyway at 3.30pm and met no opposition. By 4.15pm the battalion was consolidated on its objective. Basil and the boys would have seen a number of the enemy running away from the houses near the north of the lake with their hands up and waving white flags as the tanks fired on the houses they vacated. Enemy mortars put down a certain amount of sporadic mortar fire on the battalion position but caused no casualties and at 5.00pm as per the plan, the Irish Guards passed through them to attack Hommersum.

By 7pm the Irish Guards had captured Hommersum having met little opposition. The Welsh Guards completed the clearing of the wood but were taking casualties from land mines. In all, 49 prisoners of war had been captured. All four of the battalion's companies were at their final objective around the area of the lake where the sands end in several prominent dunes. For reasons only known to the Germans, they had clearly chosen not to make a stand on this occasion.

This attack, as detailed, barely registers in the annals of military history, particularly when more serious actions were going on to the north of them. The Canadians and British were taking heavy losses now that the Germans had arrived in force to attack and counterattack them around Kleve, and the edge of the Reichswald Forest.

To Basil and the boys this was their first 'blooding'.

Everything about the day was a first for them and must have elicited an explosion of intense emotions. They had never experienced a real attack across open ground that could so easily have turned into a killing field should the information have turned out to be wrong. They would have been aware that the Germans were known to place low trip wires triggering warning flares or land mines, particularly so in such soft ground, thus every step would have been an unbearable dice with the devil. Mercifully, it panned out more like a training exercise, but they had never witnessed the horrifying sight of bullet-ridden colleagues thrown to the ground before them in their agonised death throes. They had never been under a mortar attack and certainly never fired their Lee Enfield rifles in anger at the enemy. They had never experienced the stomach-churning fear of steeling oneself to launch into an attack, of fearing that they would be able to control themselves and resist the human desire to run or hide. They had never had to fear for their very existence or suffer disfiguring injury. But most of all, to not let their colleagues down.

The sight of seeing German soldiers for the first time, even though they were surrendering must have left a lasting impression. They must have ended the day feeling a mixture of elation, exhaustion, relief, and a massive adrenaline fuelled newfound confidence in themselves. The attack had not been without casualties, six guardsmen were wounded two of them from 4 Company. The guardsman killed by the tank's machine gun accidentally firing was from the Support Company.

Once they had consolidated the position by digging shallow 'slit' trenches for their protection against shelling and counterattack, Basil and the boys would have been able to peer over the tops of the dunes and see across the German border towards Hommersum. Where the Irish Guards had passed through virtually unopposed, the land was flat with waterlogged meadows. Isolated farmsteads were dotted around and there was very little cover from enemy fire. The sand dunes behind them, resembling multiple small but steep heather and tree clad hillocks, proved to be a huge challenge to pass supplies up to them and they had to settle down with no more than their hard rations. Sporadic mortar shells landed all around them, bursting into the soft sand and fortunately causing no further casualties. At least it wasn't raining. They had been lucky; in the next attack the battalion was going to have a far heavier price to pay.

12

The attack on the Siegfried Line

Basil and the boys awoke hungry from an uncomfortable and miserable night in their cold and damp slit trenches. A thick mist clung to the heather and thin trees all around them, penetrating their clothing and undoubtedly making them shudder. The question mark shaped lake beside them would have seemed eerie in the morning light as they and everyone around them began brewing the morning tea. The day would be spent consolidating their position by deepening their slit trenches against any potential counter-attack and preparing for the next day's attack.

The planning for that attack lasted most of the day. The battalion war diary records:

15 February
1515 Hours – The enemy appear to be very strong in Artillery. HOMMERSUM has been very heavily shelled several times today, also there are some stubborn enemy in the houses to the South and Southeast of the village.

In view of the stiffening enemy opposition the Brigade Commander proposes to alter the Battalions' objective to the section of defences South of HOMMERSUM. 1600 Hours – ……. The Battalion's objective for tomorrow was confirmed as the villages of MULL …; STARTENHOF….; and RETUT ….

So the next attack then, was to capture three villages (more fortified farmsteads and surrounding buildings) to the south of Hommersum, just south of the river Kendel where it bends dramatically in a 'U' shape. Also, the frontier post just to the south of the farmsteads. The objective was to enable Hassum to be captured and open up the road to Hommersum. It was to be the first part of an elaborate series of eight co-ordinated attacks from the north and west by various other British and Canadian troops, aimed at moving the front line closer to the large town of Goch. Basil and the boys would be supported in the attack by the Welsh Guards' tanks, anti-tank guns, machine gun teams, and the Royal Engineers.

Müll, Startenhof and Retut were not just any random farmsteads, they lay just inside the German/Dutch border and were part of the infamous Siegfried Line. Farms in the area were ideally sighted for mutually supportive defensive positions. Anti-tank guns were concealed amongst hedges, orchards and buildings, and the ground was sewn with land mines. The Germans had taken to hiding in cellars of farmhouses whilst they were being shelled, then running out to man the buildings and trenches around them. Immediate vicious counter attacks were launched when buildings were captured, by troops prepared to fight to the last man. With the German defenders arriving in ever increasing numbers the fighting was by now taking on a more bitter character.

This then is what Basil and the boys faced as they left their positions in the sand dunes, on the morning of the 16th of February, after another uncomfortable night. Through grey skies and low mist, they marched south along *Zandkuilseweg*, onto *Hommerumseweg*, and finally onto *Kamperweg* on the Dutch side of the border towards the start line of the attack. To their left, through the mist that mercifully hid them from enemy observation, they would have been able to see Hommersum, just 600 yards away, now in ruins being heavily shelled by the Germans whose artillery had dramatically increased in strength over the past few days. They would have seen the smoke and debris rising at every strike and were probably wondering how anyone could survive there.

Their previous attack had been completed without supporting artillery as it was known that the Germans had pulled back beyond their objective. This attack was however being supported by heavy artillery and mortars. Basil and the boys would have felt the percussion on their chests, their deafening fearful roar as they opened up, adding to the cacophony of sound, as they pounded the German positions. Each salvo would have shaken them to their core. The Welsh Guards were there with tanks in support of the attack also firing with the artillery.

Basil and the boys would have heard from long before they even joined up that the Siegfried Line was a formidable obstacle. They will also have been briefed that it was no longer the threat it was lorded to be as the Americans further south had already breached it and found it lacking. But everyone of their generation was aware of the Somme battle in the First World War where almost 60,000 casualties were taken in the first hour of the attack when it was thought that the German defences were destroyed and deemed no longer a threat. The ground in front of them was completely flat and very open with no cover whatsoever. There were also the ominous groups of farm buildings. Most noticeable, was that it was extremely boggy and likely that progress would be slow; like trying to walk across the boggiest of ploughed fields and the mud sticking to your feet weighing them down. There were also mines known to be laid. Whilst waiting the last agonising few minutes before the attack, one can only imagine their kaleidoscope of thoughts, ranging from the exhilaration of witnessing the magnitude of the event unfolding, to knee trembling, stomach churning fear.

The objectives for each of the forward companies were: 1 Company to attack on the right and capture the Frontier Post, and two bridges over the nearby anti-tank ditch. 4 Company were to lead the attack on the left and capture the wood north of Müll, the Müll farmstead, and the bridge over the flooded anti-tank ditch nearby. 3 Company were to then pass through 4 Company and attack the farmsteads of Startenhof and Retut. 2 Company to be in reserve.

The start line for the attack was set as being along *Kamperweg* in the area just north of the modern A57 Motorway, southwest of Hommersum. Just a small field away from the German border. The attack for Basil and 4 Company was to be directed in an easterly direction, roughly following the modern *Mortelweg*, towards Müll, keeping the river Kendel on their left. 1 Company would attack southeast towards the frontier post.

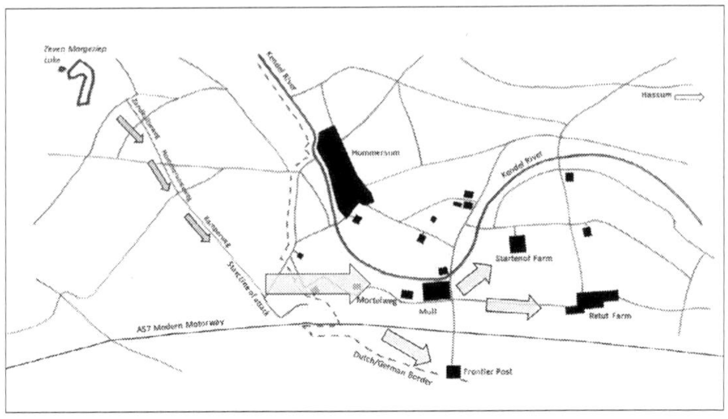

The attack on Müll, 16th February 1945

As the morning turned into afternoon, the mist cleared. At 1.30pm the attack went forward. Immediately the German artillery stopped pounding Hommersum and opened up on them with continuous fire. Basil and the boys were moving steadily forward, bayonets fixed, heads down, trudging and squelching through the clinging heavy mud. Their ears deafened from their own artillery behind them and the explosions all around them throwing up huge fountains of mud, soaking them, and filling their nostrils with hot acrid cordite fumes. As the ground was so soft, the shells and mortar rounds were largely burying themselves and mercifully minimising the murderous showers of shrapnel. To their left was the river Kendel now swollen to 50 yards wide. Ahead of them they would be able to see their shells landing, causing white mushroom shaped smoke and flashes of explosions as they hit their intended targets. They would be able to see the farmhouses they were heading towards on fire with billowing smoke pouring off the tileless roofs. The ominous and terrifying rapid rattle of the German machine guns opening up on them must have been terrifying. Beside them the tanks were getting into difficulty and all but two of them became hopelessly bogged down and unable to follow the attack, leaving them to cross the open ground unprotected. To their right, 1 Company were taking casualties from a nearby machine gun post and Basil and the boys would likely have seen them falling.

Crossing the open fields Basil and 4 Company came across haystacks that turned out to be concrete enemy pill boxes so disguised. Mercifully, these were unmanned. They pressed on and came under intense rifle and machine gun fire from the buildings ahead. They rapidly cleared the wood and the buildings of determined defenders using grenades, bayonets, and rifles, and then onto the flooded anti-tank ditch and the bridge over it. They were coming under intense fire from the buildings across the river Kendel to their left. Part of the company rushed across the causeway over the badly damaged bridge and crossed single file to the other side under what turned out to be inaccurate fire from the buildings. They then stormed the buildings killing any that dared to oppose them and causing the remainder to retreat in disarray.

The exhausting mud hampered 'charge' across the flat fields, the bloody house clearances, sweeping of the woods, capture of the flooded anti-tank ditch, and the epic storming of the river crossing took an hour and a half. 4 Company held their position and allowed 3 Company to pass through them and across their prized bridge over the flooded anti-tank ditch, onward for their attack on Startenhof and Retut. Basil and boys would have been able to watch them getting smaller and smaller as they made their muddy way across the fields towards the farmsteads a few hundred yards away.

To their right 1 Company were in trouble. They had captured the frontier post but were unable to capture the anti-tank ditch bridge nearby as the enemy put up a sustained defence. 3 Company eventually captured the two remaining farmsteads of Startenhof and Retut, and by 4.30pm Battalion HQ was set up in the largest farmhouse, all positions now consolidated. Basil, George, Mansel, Paul and Fred had done it. The battalion had done it. They had broken into the Siegfried Line and were now standing on German soil.

Many of the deaths and injuries in the battalion attack had been the result of the sustained and accurate shelling as they crossed the open ground, but now the shelling was directed onto the positions they were holding and was increasing in intensity. The shelling made it an incredibly dangerous place to be and so the task for Basil and 4 Company was to 'dig in' as fast as they knew how. The red hot shrapnel sizzling over their prostrate bodies would have forced them to bury their faces and wriggle like maggots to get further down to avoid the horror. The exploding shells would have made the ground shake and send up huge fountains of mud, falling down and trying to bury them where they lay. Being shelled must have been a terrifying experience but they had to prepare themselves as best they could, as the Germans were now sending over smoke canisters, a known indication to anticipate an imminent counterattack. It never came but they continued to shell the battalion positions until midnight when the other co-ordinated attacks went in on either side of them and to the north of Goch. The guns then turned their attention to those attacks, giving Basil and the boys some respite.

They were all caked in mud and soaked to the skin. With the river Kendel in full flood, the water table was barely below the surface meaning that their shallow trenches were full of icy-cold filthy water. To make matters worse, it rained; the cold drizzle sizzling on the burnt out buildings behind them, steam rising from the charred rafters. The rain turned the ground they had attacked over into a quagmire making it a laborious, painfully slow task to get hot food and supplies to them. They were eventually fed sometime after midnight. Those not on watch duty may have managed to get some sleep out of sheer exhaustion but mid-February in northern Europe is extremely cold at night and thus Basil and the boys must have had an unbearably uncomfortable night in the open, either inside the destroyed roofless buildings or around them in their hellish slit trenches. It would have been pitch black, with the sky flickering like firework displays on three sides of them. The rumble of the guns not very far away would have been their backdrop. The causeway that the Royal Engineers had hastily built for the tanks to cross the anti-tank ditch was swept away by the floods in the night.

The attack cost the battalion the lives of 13 men and 27 wounded, amazingly none of them from 4 Company. They had taken 154 prisoners of war and captured various guns and ammunition. The brave, experienced, and tenacious German defenders at Müll were the 122nd Grenadier Regiment (part of the 180th Infantry Division). This regiment had suffered badly from previous fighting and were perhaps no longer the potent force they were six months before, but they still put up a strong resistance. It is not recorded how many of their number were killed or wounded.

First light on the Siegfried Line, on the morning of the 17th of February must have seemed surreal. All of the noise and carnage of yesterday was replaced by misty silence and there would have been little sign of life. Everyone in the forward Companies were 'dug in', fatigued, soaking wet, caked in mud and cold to the bone. For Basil and the boys, it must have been a deep low point compared to the mad exhilaration mixed with expectation of death experienced the previous day and night. There was no opportunity to change into dry clothes, they had to hold the position against counterattacks for at least a few days.

During the day, 1 Company managed to capture the bridge that had eluded them the day before and captured three snipers that had been inflicting casualties. They had professed that their group had withdrawn in the night after suffering heavy casualties. The rain grew heavier and lasted throughout the next night. Basil and the boys, drenched, half frozen and mud-caked, had to just tough it out in the most miserable of freezing cold conditions. Semi amphibious 'Weasels' now had to be used to bring up the hot meals and supplies.

At 4.30am on Monday the 19th February, an enemy patrol silently infiltrated their position, right into the middle of 4 Company. There ensued a fearful firefight in the pitch dark. The confusion and chaos must have been absolute. Basil and the boys must have fired off every round they had and resigned themselves to hand-to-hand fighting. Mercifully it is not documented that it came to that, but it lasted an hour and resulted in one of 4 Company's platoon commanders –

Lieutenant G.D. Wauhope being seriously wounded before the attackers withdrew.

This experience would have set the tone for the many future occasions when Basil and the boys would find themselves on the front line with nothing between them and the enemy. The constant fear of enemy counterattack or patrols penetrating their lines must have caused as much strain on the nerves and senses than the shelling and the terrible weather conditions, leading to sleepless nervous exhaustion. The long winter nights would be of intense darkness, interspersed with brilliant flashes of gunfire and explosions, the brightness temporarily blinding them and the cacophony of sound deafening their ears. This being interspersed with periods of absolute silence between salvos. It must have induced constant terror, way beyond our peacetime imagination as they lay there in their putrid slit trenches straining their eyes and ears to any sound or movement that could be the enemy creeping up on them and so death.

At 1130 am a heavy and accurate bombardment came down on the anti-tank ditch crossing right next to where the boys were surviving like automatons. It was suspected that there might be a connection between the bombardment and the patrol of last night, and that there might be someone directing the fire from the houses in no-man's land, which were accordingly fired on with machine guns. This flushed out one German who was trying to desert. It transpired that he was the commanding officer's servant, and a member of last night's patrol. The patrol was 25 strong led by a sergeant and had been given the mission of recapturing some of the arms and ammunition that they had left behind in the buildings occupied by 4 Company. They failed to do this and the patrol returned to find that four were missing presumed wounded.

The next day, at 9.00pm a patrol from 2 Company were ambushed at the Frontier Post. The enemy opened fire at them from a house on the left of the road at very close range, killing the patrol commander and wounding another of the patrol who was captured.

The following day the Irish Guards launched an attack just to their south from the area of the frontier post. It was a similar style attack as the one Basil and the boys had successfully completed but they took over 200 casualties and had to be withdrawn whilst 1 Company held the line at the anti-tank bridge to cover their withdrawal. How easily this could have been the fate of Basil's attack. There is a lot of luck in war. During that night Basil and the boys came under intermittent attack from mortar fire and shellfire from a self-propelled gun.

Finally, on the morning of the 22nd of February, after seven of the (as yet) most uncomfortable, appallingly terrifying days and nights, Basil and the boys were told they were to move out of the Siegfried Line and back to Hommersum village, leaving their hideously uncomfortable hell holes to the Scots Guards. The battalion had sustained another ten casualties since the initial attack, mainly from shell fire. The relief must have been incredible but the sights awaiting them must have staggered them. Hommersum was in ruins, barely a building was left standing amongst the filthy pools of flood water. The roads were churned with shell craters, numerous smashed military vehicles of all types could be seen on the sides of roads having struck land mines. Telephone poles were smashed and lines trailing all around. The church had received multiple hits and the graveyard a fearsome sight with many graves being blown around by shell fire, with disinterred body fragments laying around on the surface amongst the smashed gravestones. The rooms in the badly damaged schoolhouse were scattered with straw and looked like they had been used by the German troops prior to their departure. The cellars in some of the buildings offered a measure of protection from the weather and were at least dry.

There to meet them was a mobile shower unit with a 'Heath Robinson' shower system. The sight of naked guardsmen frolicking under the mist of soapy steam and spurts of hot water from overhead sprinklers must have been a sight not to be unseen. To follow that were fresh supplies of clean underwear, socks and shirts that must have felt heavenly after the filthy attire they had been wearing. Being the elite Coldstream Guards that they were, they would have spent that afternoon doing everything possible to clean themselves up. Scraping off the mud, brushing their uniforms, shaving, polishing kit, and being inspected. It must have been the Coldstream Guards' *Second to none* discipline and training that held them together through that week. And of course, the bond between them that only people who have suffered a collective experience such as that can have.

Soldiers have described this bond as being way beyond just friendship, more a love of their fellows, whom they trusted their lives to, and would give their lives for. Most would never again experience this kind of love. Right from the start of their training the trust of their fellows was engendered, such that they would be able second guess their respective reactions. This trust, together with supporting each other through terrible experiences and absolute terror led to that love. Soldiers who experienced combat for the first time explain that the biggest battle they had to face was with themselves, their biggest fear being of letting their fellows down.

They were allowed one night's rest and must have slept the sleep of the dead. Meanwhile, Goch had finally been captured from sustained attacks from the north at a high price in lives lost.

13

Buchholt

For Basil and the battalion, the capture of Goch marked the end of their attachment to the 51st Highland Division for on the 23rd of February they were returned to the Guards Armoured Division but now placed under the command of the 5th Guards Armoured Brigade, alongside the 1st Battalion Coldstream Guards in their Sherman Tanks.

They were ordered to take over an area around the small village of Buchholt, northeast of Goch, which had been captured the day before when the Goch to Kalkar road was cut. The battalion's job was to hold the position and defend against any counterattack. Retaining the Goch to Kalkar road was important as it was a significant supply route for the British and Canadians, as it had been for the Germans.

At 7.30pm the battalion left Hommersum and were transported in troop carrying lorries via Gennep, Kessel, Asperden, and Goch. Basil and the boys would have noticed from peering out of the truck that for the first time many of the houses were displaying white sheets as flags from the windows. Particularly harrowing for Basil and Mansel with their farming background would have been the common sight of livestock left wandering the fields, mewing sadly as their bloated udders went un-milked, and others chained to their stalls awaiting their sad fate, their owners nowhere to be seen.

From Goch they continued to the crossroads on the Goch to Kalkar road, at its junction with *Keppelnerstraße*, arriving at 11.30pm. From the crossroads the companies marched through the driving rain to the battalion position in pitch darkness whilst the vehicles remained parked near the crossroads. Owing to the nature of their new position it was only possible to get vehicles up to the companies by night, as they were under observation from the Germans on the next ridge and any movement would be liable to bring down a great deal of accurate shelling. The poor roads and tracks leading to the companies were only passable in bren-gun carriers and jeeps, and so those were used to carry the company rations, blankets etc off the battle wagons. A nightly carrier convoy was set up to supply the companies with their hot food, ammunition, etc.

When nearing their new positions, they must have had to maintain silence, but blundering their way along in the pitch dark amongst the Scots Guards they were relieving must have led to many sour muttered utterances. Basil and the boys spent the rest of the night around the semi destroyed farm buildings in a completely unfamiliar location. I doubt anyone slept that night. They were in fact lined up to the north of the village along *Kühnenstraße* in and around Kühnenhof farm. The Support Company and Battalion HQ were just to their left, 2 Company to their right, with 1 and 3 Companies to their rear in and around the village. Two large field guns, and a mortar section were next to them, which must have been deafening every time they fired off salvos.

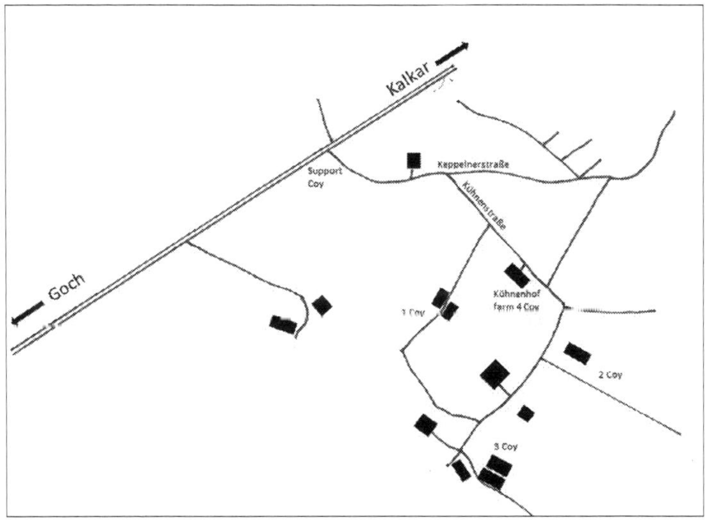

5th Battalion positions north-east of Goch, 24th February 1945

At first light and in the cold chill of dawn, Basil and the boys would have been able to see the extent of the position they were holding. They were on a slope in full view of the enemy, once again in boggy saturated ground looking out on cold wintery shell battered fields. In front of them were a scattering of farms and houses towards the village of Halvenboom. The air reeked of burned and decomposing cattle. The farm buildings around them were in ruins with livestock tethered in their stalls where they had burned to death, the owners having been evacuated to Bedburg-Hau camp near Kleve which was by then behind the Allied front line. Around them were dead livestock with bloated balloon like bodies with legs splayed out sideways. Amongst them lucky survivors were randomly grazing where they could. To add to the squalor, in the midst of 4 Company's position, they would have all been able to watch as a badly wounded pig ate from the corpse of what had once been a horse.

Worst of all, any movement in daylight would have brought shells raining on them so motionless they had to lay in the icy mud for hours on end. It must have been the most depressing situation, having just endured a week of exposure to the elements and enemy gunfire, they were again to spend more extremely uncomfortable days and nights enduring whatever the enemy and the weather threw at them. There was little or no cover from enemy shells and mortars which rained down that afternoon on the Support Company and Battalion HQ to their left, causing casualties. Later the enemy turned their attention on to the area where Basil and the boys were laying.

The mortars were worse than the shells, with their near vertical trajectory they were able to fall vertically over their parapets, making a doleful crump sound as they entered the saturated earth. Most terrifying of all were the nebelwerfers, known by the troops as 'moaning minis' or 'sobbing sisters' and were multi-rocket powered mortars which produced glowing trails of sparks in an arc accompanied by a characteristic 'moan' followed by loud 'crumps' as the carpet of explosions devastated their targeted area. Heavy shelling went on during the early part of the night before things quietened down again.

It's hard for us to imagine now just how men coming under such a barrage could possibly feel whilst we are in the security of peacetime, warm and dry in the comfort of home with no obvious threat to life. From those soldiers who have tried to describe their ordeals, it is clear that it is almost beyond their words. From their collective experiences, in order to appreciate just a hint of what it must have been like, you would have to imagine enduring the noise and the tumult of earth as the incoming enemy fire strikes home, hang onto a dwindling supply of luck, and listen for the tell-tale tone of the shell that will kill or hideous maim you from a direct hit. You would have to imagine tasting the pungent smoke and cordite in your mouth and nostrils. To imagine the ear-splitting crescendo of thunderous sound from field artillery and mortar teams behind you, masking the sound of incoming fire, thus inducing the absolute blind terror that every unheard incoming shell could be the one. To imagine hearing the agonised cries of those around you wounded by enormous shell fragments. All this whilst maintaining an abhorrent lonely existence in a virtual readymade grave half full of almost freezing filthy water.

Keeping below the ground level was clearly the only way to hopefully survive a bombardment. Digging holes was always a muddy, backbreaking pastime. Invariably the bottom of the 'foxhole' filled with cold, icy water, or in warm weather attracted swarms of mosquitos to torment them. Almost always they provided the most uncomfortable cramped sleeping arrangement but far preferable to lying on the surface and being hideously wounded or killed by mortar fire that could come at any time without warning. Where possible they lined the bottom with straw to provide some reprieve from a soaking wet and cold miserable night. When having to dig in under trees they quickly learned to cover their foxhole with tree trunks as mortar rounds exploded overhead on contact with the high branches caused far more casualties. Every overnight stop entailed 'digging in'.

For Basil and the battalion and indeed all infantrymen, the strategic decisions, and the plans of attack were known only to those at high level. They had no idea of the 'big picture', on many occasions no idea of even where the enemy were. The enemy could be either miles away or as close as the next building. This constant lack of knowledge invariably caused unnecessary tension and strained nerves, making a priority for every stop to dig in and post a 24 hour watch. The general life of an infantryman meant a constant and continuous feeling of intense fatigue. The dreaded order "prepare to move" always meant an end to a miserable night but signified a resumption of the stomach churning fear of the next unknown.

With the conditions as bad as they were, hot rations would have been few and far between for the forward companies. The standard army rations delivered via the carriers were those contained in a box with enough food for fourteen men for 24 hours. It contained tinned foods (mostly soya-link sausages, bacon, baked beans, biscuits, soup, bread, compo tea, cigarettes, and a few sheets of toilet roll per man). One of the empty biscuit tins would be filled with soil and petrol poured in. This would act as a reasonably effective cooker to warm the food and boil water for tea. The tea would have been tainted with the chlorine from the water tanks but could be just palatable if the powdered tea were added just before boiling so that the milk powder didn't congeal but still allowed for the tea to brew. The box the food came in was often used as a makeshift toilet by cutting a hole in the lid. The box then sunk into a hole prepared in the ground.

Laying there, cold, wet and shivering, with time to stare up at skies filled with American bomber vapour trails by day and the RAF bombers occasionally just visible in the moonlight at night, all flying to and from England, I can't help wondering if Basil's thoughts turned to home. Of his mum Lillian, his brothers Ken and Gordon, of sisters Hazel, Mary, Iris and Vera. Of his retriever bitch, 'Floss'. Of sitting in front of the flickering kitchen fire. Seeing the awful state of the farm they occupied must have made him think about Farrant's farm, of Jack Miller, of Mr Farrant, of the neatly ploughed and well drained fields, the dairy heard, the plough horses, and life in warm dry clothes. War ravaged Germany must have seemed a million miles from home. His life now was the battalion, the company and his close mates, George, Mansel, Paul and Fred.

14

Life back home

Back home, again nothing much had changed. Village life was very far removed from the war raging in Germany and the far east. Rationing had become progressively tedious and the main subject of most people's conversation. Bread was never rationed so breakfast was almost always toast and jam, or dripping. The hand cut slices were dangled on a toasting fork over the open range, often falling off into the embers and having to be retrieved and dusted off to start again.

Iris went to Botley School, so she walked Vera to Cumnor School, then caught the free double decker bus outside the school to Botley School and back in the afternoon. Lunch was invariably jam sandwiches made by Lillian to take with them. Lillian would stoke up the range fire before cooking tea, usually sausages and mash, or mince and dumplings. Rabbit stew and dumplings was often eaten, as they were generally easy to obtain from locals who trapped or chased them out with ferrets. They could usually be brought for 1 shilling from the door at Waistie's farm across the 'Closes' field. After the last harvest, rabbits were plentiful and were shot as they ran away from the corn sheafs, but a new harvest was still some months away. Lillian always skinned and butchered the rabbits. The chickens at the bottom of the garden produced eggs and the big old cooking apple tree supplied them with apples to go in pies for months. Although there was a village shop, food orders were taken weekly, along with the ration cards, by a boy on a bicycle working for the International Food Store in High Street Oxford. The orders were then later delivered by van. The milkman, Mr Bishop, who was a relation of Lillian's sister, delivered the milk on a horse and cart. He used to be able to make a click noise in his mouth and the horse knew to walk on to the next stop without him being near it. The fishmonger came once per week in a van, as did paraffin deliveries.

On the 20th of February, as they gathered around the old wood framed radio, the BBC announced that the British and Canadian 1st Army had captured the Siegfried Line just west of Goch. Also, that a portion of the Goch-Kalkar road had been secured within two miles of Kalkar.'

Lillian could not have known that Basil was there, miserably exposed to the elements and the enemy. Or that within a few days he would be off to that awful, exposed hillside at Buchholt, to hold onto that Goch – Kalkar road, to provide a firm base and ward off counterattacks in such squalid conditions.

15

Operation Blockbuster

Operation Grenade, the American part of the 'pincer' movement, intended to be launched at the same time or shortly after Operation Veritable never actually got under way until the 23rd of February, once the floods on the river Roer had subsided sufficiently to make a crossing possible. By this time many of the German troops had moved north to defend against the British-Canadian attack. The American 9th Army were therefore able to make progress towards the Rhine and northward towards the Rhine bridges at Wesel. Given that Operation Veritable was originally planned to take just four days to capture them, and after more than two weeks they were barely halfway there, a revised plan was called for.

This revised plan was named Operation Blockbuster and was to be launched on the 26th of February. It required, the Canadians to clear the flooded areas along the Rhine, whilst British forces attack southeast through the German second line of defences known as the 'Hockwald Layback' and other key positions to the south. The Guards Armoured Division, of which Basil was a part of, would then take over and attack towards the bridges at Wesel whilst other British troops covered their flank and met the Americans approaching from the south. (See map of Operation Veritable)

Basil and the battalion's return to the Guards Armoured Division and their move to hold the line at Buchholt had been prompted by the American 9th Army's crossing of the river Roer and the planning of Operation Blockbuster.

On the muddy hillside at Buchholt, the morning of the 25th saw the artillery pieces around them, and many others all along the line firing an almost continuous head splitting barrage. Conversely, the enemy were quieter than usual, but started shelling the forward companies in the afternoon, and went on till late at night when two self-propelled guns fired on their positions. A house occupied by Support Company received a direct hit causing several casualties.

The following morning Operation Blockbuster was launched. At 4am Basil and the boys would have been awoken from their cold fitful slumber, soaked and with teeth chattering, to witness the familiar clattering, grinding and squealing noise of tanks approaching them from behind. As they came nearer their vibrations would be felt through the ground as the soil from the top of their slit trenches fell onto them.

This was the advance through them of the 3rd Canadian Division and the 11th Armoured Division on route to their objectives. It must have been an awesome sight watching the flickering shadowy shapes of the long lines of infantry following along behind the tanks, lit by the flashes of gunfire against the backdrop of the dull red sky illuminated by distant Typhoon rocket attacks. The small town of Uedem burned ahead of them as the tiny specks of khaki figures interspersed with dirty black spurts of smoke made steady progress down the hillside and up over the crest amid the cacophony of sound from the big guns.

They were now safe in the knowledge that there were now troops and massed armoured vehicles between them and the enemy. That must have, at least for a short time, left them at peace with the world. The attack was highly successful with the towns of Keppeln, Kalkar and Uedem being captured.

During the day and most of the night the enemy continued to put down shells in the battalion area, but with the capture of Uedem in the early hours of the 27th, there was peace and quiet for the remainder of their time at Buchholt. The front had now moved forward leaving them on the exposed muddy hillside to dwell on their misery, discomfort and exhaustion. Basil and the boys from all the rifle companies were able to have rest periods in the houses and farm buildings in their areas, and though they were all very damaged, were thankfully able to find some cover from the elements and an opportunity to dry out and gain some warmth from their improvised fires.

Whilst the boys were at Buchholt they were shown a personal message sent from General Horrocks, it read:

"Personal from Commander 30 CORPS to all troops. You have taken approximately 12,000 Prisoners of War and killed large numbers of Germans. You have broken through the Siegfried Line and drawn on to yourselves the bulk of the German reserves in the WEST. A strong U.S. offensive was launched over the ROER at 0330

hours this morning against positions which thanks to your efforts are lightly held by the Germans. Thank you for what you have done so well."

The Battalion's price for holding the line at Buchholt amounted to one guardsman killed and nineteen wounded, three of which were from 4 Company.

16

Metzekath

From their capture of Müll until leaving Buchholt they had endured almost three weeks of exposure to some of the worst winter weather for many years, and all the 'hate' the enemy could muster in the form of artillery, mortar and nebelwerfer bombardment. They had lain in small hastily dug shallow pits not long enough to stretch out and half full of icy cold water for hours at a time, enduring unimaginable deprivation devoid of life's basic comforts, and suffering the intense pains of cramp. This superhuman feat of endurance should have been rewarded with a long rest and recuperation period, but as per the plan, the battalion were to be needed for the final phase of Blockbuster, a series of attacks towards the Wesel Bridges.

On the 4th of March they were driven in TCLs straight from Buchholt to the ruins of Goch where they formed up behind the 1st Battalion Coldstreams in their Sherman tanks. At midnight, under the eerie light of 'Monty's moonlight' (consisting of powerful spotlights bounced off clouds) they drove off to join the battle now raging near the Bönninghardt Ridge. The route taken from Goch passed through the small towns of Weeze, a surprisingly undamaged Kevelaer, and Wetten. They stopped for breakfast at 7am, a few miles east of Wetten. The battalion was then further transported to the small town of Kapellen where they stopped just short of the outskirts before the bridge over the Issumer Flueth stream. It had been blown by the retreating Germans and in the process of being replaced by a Bailey bridge. Nearby to their left were a series of connected small lakes.

There they would have seen the impressive sight of the 1st Battalion Coldstream Guards' Sherman tanks massed either side of the road, jockeying for parking places, together with at least eight batteries of artillery firing with an unearthly noise towards the Bönninghardt Ridge in the near distance. The barrels flashing and recoiling, wheels bouncing amid billowing smoke as the gunners rammed in round after round, each making a loud crack followed by a withering shriek together with a thunderous echo. To the left of the road was a large dwelling being set up as the Divisional Headquarters (Haus Wankum).

The Bönninghardt Ridge is in effect a five mile long densely fir tree clad hill, and forms the high ground after which to the east is a gentle slope down towards the Rhine and the Wesel Bridges. Between the ridge and the river runs the Xanten to Rheinberg road which was part of the main supply routes for the Germans. On top of the ridge within a large clearing in the trees is Metzekath. 'Kath' is a local meaning for a farm. The farm consisted of two groups of buildings either side of *Hamber Straße* (Kapellen road on war maps). The Bönninghardt Ridge and particularly the Metzekath buildings were therefore clearly a strategic position the Germans could not afford to lose possession of. It was the only high ground in front of the Rhine to their rear, and it protected their supply routes. Hitler had ordered them to not give ground and to fight to the last man. The buildings were hastily fortified, and an anti-tank gun positioned in front of the buildings with a direct view down *Hamber straße*, with sandbag and trench line defences. This was supported by two other artillery pieces and two self propelled guns. Basil and the boys may not have been told but the Germans had just doubled the strength of their forces on the ridge, mostly by the elite 8th Parachute Division. The job of taking it from them was given to the battalion. The job of clearing the Metzekath buildings to the right of *Hamber straße* was given to Basil and the boys of 4 Company. The assembly area was to be the start line for the attack.

The War Diary states:

Information: The BONNINGHARDT woods are being strongly held by units of 8 Para Division, who have been putting up a very stubborn opposition. They are being aided by several Self Propelled Guns. On the flanks, SONSBECK is still held by the enemy and 53 DIVISION have been pushed back to ISSUM by a counter attack.

Intention: 5th Battalion COLDSTREAM GUARDS will attack and capture METXEKATH…. (modern spelling now Metzekath)

Method: The Battalion will form up behind the east edge of the WOOD at 084324. Start Line the forward edge of the WOOD. Inter Company boundary and axis of advance the track from 084324 up to METXEKATH.

The Battalion will attack with two Companies up:-

Right 4 Company objective the buildings in the area 096324.

Left 3 Company objective the WOOD 097326 up to the ridge at 097328.

1 Company will follow up behind 3 Company, objective BUIDINGS at 095327.

2 Company will follow up behind 4 Company, objective BUILDINGS at 095325.

Fire Plan: 5 Field Batteries and 3 Medium Batteries will be firing a series of five progressive stinks from H to H plus 29.

A Section of Mortars will move with each forward Company.

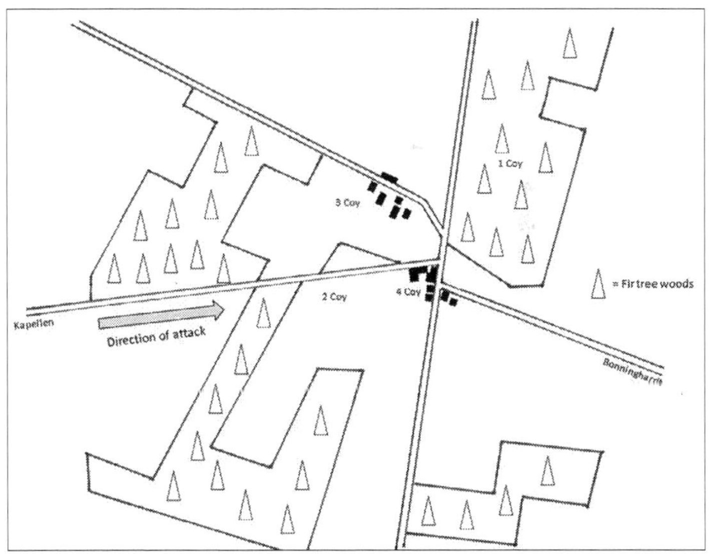

Battalion positions after attack on Metzekath, 9th March 1945

*Admin: …… Greatcoats, a blanket, and the evening
meal will come up on the Carriers after consolidation.
Intercommunications: Battalion H.Q. will move down
the track and will then establish itself at 095327.*

The dense fir trees precluded any effective use of tanks
so the attack was to be purely an infantry affair with only
artillery in support. The low cloud cover prevented any air
support that could be provided by Hawker Typhoons and
their devastating rockets. The 1st Battalion Coldstream tanks
were to remain idly at Kapellen until the 11th of March, but
with some being used for subsequent attacks. This proved a
period of light relief for them, with them having time to have
fun boating on the lake in canoes and punts. More sombrely,
they were to find that houses in Kapellen had been looted by
the retreating German troops. They were also to find many
Russian slave labourers and some German civilians, all in
poor condition and in need of help.

It was now gone 3pm. From Kapellen, Basil and the boys
would have seen the smoke and noise of battle raging at the
edge of the woods at the base of the ridge where the Grenadiers
were attacking and where the artillery rounds were falling. That
was to be their assembly area for the attack. The battalion set to
and marched there. They passed through the centre of Kapellen
and its dishevelled looted houses, with remnants of everyday
household items and belongings of the owners' strewn around
them. Once clear of the town they marched into open ground
along *Gelderner straße* and into *Gruneuwaldweg* where they
halted near its junction with *Hamber straße*. They were now
at the base of the Bönninghardt Ridge with the dense woods
ahead of them. There they waited.

'The battalion's attack was planned for 5pm but this was delayed until 5.30pm until the Grenadiers had finally overcome very stiff opposition to secure the start line for their attack. The time delay no doubt straining Basil and the boys' nerves to the very limit. That same knee shaking, vomit inducing tension. At 5.30pm sharp, five field batteries and three medium batteries from the artillery they had seen at Kapellen opened up in support of the attack. The artillery rounds, like a thousand express trains roared over their heads towards their target making the ground shake as they thundered into the buildings and surrounding ground ahead of them. One of the artillery pieces dropped short of their target and a whole salvo crashed directly onto the start line killing several of their comrades and wounding many more in front of their eyes. The boys had to again steal themselves from this horrific scene of carnage as the attack was not to be halted. They had to cover about a mile of ground through the dark and dense pine woods alongside and to the right of *Hamber straße*. They left the carnage behind them and wound their way through the trees, bayonets fixed and hand grenades in their pockets. A mortar team followed them as per the plan. To their left the battalion's HQ Company tank clattered along *Hamber straße* beside them. After it had gone only a few yards there was an explosion as the tank hit a land mine, putting it out of action and blocking the road. A few minutes later one of the HQ Company's Bren-gun carriers met the same fate. They pressed on regardless, 3 Company kept pace with them through the trees on the other side of the road, with 1 Company behind them. The enemy were in the woods firing at them from hidden positions, but the momentum and ferocity of their attack overwhelmed them with only a few casualties.

When Basil and 4 Company reached the edge of the wood they could see their objective, the farm buildings some 150 yards across open upward-sloping shell pocked ground. In front of the buildings they saw what was a 7.5 Pak anti-tank gun, with the sandbag and trench line defences. They could also see the two self-propelled artillery guns nearby, together with what was an 88mm artillery gun and a French anti-tank gun all supported by a strong infantry presence. As soon as the enemy sighted them on the edge of the woods, the large artillery guns opened fire on them at near point-blank range with everything they had. The enemy infantry fired at them with machine guns, anti-tank rounds from panzerfausts (bazookas), and mortars directly into the tree line; their only cover. Basil and the boys were halted in their tracks. The corporal in charge of the mortar team was killed instantly by an anti-tank round. At this point one of 4 Company's platoon commanders, Lieutenant Michael Wall, took decisive action to have a smoke canister fired from a mortar to provide a smokescreen between them and the enemy position. Led by Lieutenant Wall; Basil, Mansel, Paul, George, and Fred and all of 4 Company then charged towards the anti-tank gun position. With hearts pounding from the exertion and wild eyed, they raced over the shell pocked ground whilst bullets and panzerfaust projectiles whistled around them, fired by the desperate defenders. Like madmen they plunged into the smokescreen and stormed into the defences killing all the gun crew and infantry with bayonets, grenades and gunfire, one bayoneted whilst bravely attempting to reload the gun. Keeping the momentum going they raced into the shell shattered farm buildings a few yards further on where every one of the enemy met the same bloody end. The remaining artillery positions were overwhelmed, and the two self-propelled guns melted away to fight another day.

These were battle-hardened, brave men of the elite Parachute Division who found themselves in an impossible position, with no opportunity to retreat from a superior force, fighting hand to hand to the last man as per their order direct from Adolf Hitler. When the attack swept through to the buildings at the rear, the defenders, who were from lesser German units finally gave up and surrendered. 3 Company and 1 Company's assault was equally successful to their left. It was all over in two hours and the Metzekath and the ridge were in the possession of the battalion. 109 prisoners of war were taken. It is unknown how many of the German defenders were killed or wounded. The swift and decisive attack proved to be devastating to the Germans who pulled back in a disorganised state resulting in very little shelling of the position after capture.

During the night a large number of enemy troops were seen by 1 Company, but they withdrew after being fired on, and an enemy patrol was also fired at. The battle continued by others to the north but for now all they had to do was dig in and let others take over the advance the next day. The Germans were slowly being squeezed into an ever decreasing hemispherical pocket in front of the Rhine bridges at Wesel.

This attack had been even more brutal than the attack on Müll. One can only wonder how it feels to have gone through such an experience. I had intended to try and link my own experiences of policing public disorder incidents but no one in peace time can ever come close to how it must feel to come face to face with the enemy, knowing that your only chance of survival is to kill or be killed. Soldiers who have fought in combat all say that they were utterly terrified throughout the whole experience.

Several bravery medals were won that day. Basil, George, Mansel, Paul and Fred were right there beside Lieutenant Michael Wall during the bloody charge for which he was awarded a Military Cross. It was almost always the case that the officer involved received the medal on behalf of the men under his command. The cost of this bravery to the battalion was at least fourteen dead and many more wounded.

17

The Wesel Pocket – the battle for Haus Loo

By the beginning of March, the German position was steadily shrinking from the American and British-Canadian attacks. Ordered by Hitler not to retreat across the Rhine over the bridges at Wesel they had no choice but to form a defence west of the Rhine. This was effectively a hemispherical defensive line centred on the Wesel bridges utilising the remaining high ground in front of it and flooded areas to the north, with the Rhine behind them. The attack on Metzekath had assisted in reducing this line and concentrated the German forces and weaponry into a confined area, which history now refers to as the 'Wesel Pocket'. Their artillery was so densely packed and provided such effective air cover that allied Typhoon fighter bombers were unable to come close enough to launch their devastating rocket attacks. The only main supply route to the German defenders in their defensive pocket was over the Wesel rail bridge and the nearby road bridge. The road bridge runs direct to the town of Alpen. Before it reaches Alpen, the road crosses the main road from Xanten to Rheinberg thus making this a highly strategic crossroads for them. If the crossroads was captured or the Xanten to Rheinberg road cut then any supplies to forward troops would be cut off, as would any chance of their retreat across the Rhine. Their main defence of this crossroads was a large, elegant house with a ruined medieval moated earthworks in front of it, hastily fortified to become a veritable fortress. It was, and still is, known as 'Haus Loo'.

Basil and the boys would have been able to see the Xanten to Rheinberg road to the northeast from their position at Metzekath, across the flat ground, with the Rhine in the background. Haus Loo was soon to feature profoundly in their lives.

The morning of the 6th of March saw other Guards battalions attacking east from Metzekath, either side of the *Bönninghardter straße* towards the village of Bönninghardt, taking large numbers of prisoners of war. The battalion moved out of Metzekath to allow this attack to take place. After the attack they moved into undamaged farm buildings just down the *Bönninghardter straße* and found, to their surprise, twenty-six Germans hiding in the lofts who surrendered themselves. They then took over the farm as their billets for the next couple of days.

By the following morning Bönninghardt village had been captured by the Welsh Guards, who found the opposition was stiffening again, but at least the high ground overlooking the wide curve of the Rhine was now in their hands. Hitler re-issued the order that the bridgehead in front of the Wesel bridges would be held to the last man.

In the meantime, Basil's 4 Company, together with 2

Company, were given the job of clearing the large woods to the south of their position off the *Bönninghardter straße*. 'Clearing the woods' sounds like a minor event when recorded in the war diary but if you could put yourself in Basil and the boys' shoes this event must have been adrenaline fuelled and tinged with intense fear in the knowledge that only luck or their animal-like lightening reactions could save them from deadly ambush. The front line was far from secure and enemy units were still roaming around, some wanting to surrender, but some with every intention of fighting to the last man. In the woods opportunities for the enemy to ambush would have been multifarious, thus focussing their thoughts as they stepped silently on the soft pine needle coated ground in the oppressive silence of the pine scented wood, with only far off sounds of battle as a backdrop. They would have crept through the trees in the well practised straight line as per beaters at a pheasant shoot but stooped to minimise their profile, stopping every 25 yards to look around and listen intently. Their senses would have been tuned to the tell tail signs of enemy activity ahead such as disturbed ground, recent footprints, birds being disturbed, recently discarded cigarettes, ration tins and other debris of human existence in the hope that they would spot the enemy before being snuffed out from invisible positions ahead. Mercifully, they cleared the wood without incident but as they emerged the other side into open ground they came across minefields.

Minefields had been in place across many of the areas they had fought over, causing many of the battalion casualties and thus making every last one of them infinitely cautious when aware of their presence. These were left for the sappers to deal with but there were other well practiced ways of removing them, the most common was the use of one of the 'funnies' the 'Crab' or Flail tank, with its chain flail on the front to set off the mines harmlessly in front of the vehicle. There were several types of mines in common use by German forces. 'Teller' mines specifically designed to destroy armoured vehicles were extensively used. Less common but designed to generate fear were the 'Rachet' type mines that allowed several vehicles to pass over before exploding. The terrifying anti-personnel 'S' Mine, consisted of a canister sunk into the ground with three pin sized prongs, which if touched sent an inner cannister into the air at chest height where it exploded large ball bearings in all directions. 'Schu' mines were another deadly type of anti-personnel mine that were very difficult to locate as they consisted of a small wooden box commonly made by school children at school.

It was planned that the American forces would attack Haus Loo and the crossroads from the south on the morning of the 8th of March and if successful, the Guards Armoured Division would not take part in any further operations west of the Rhine.

Plans were made just in case the American attack failed. This plan was for the 52nd Lowland Division to capture the small town of Alpen, Haus Loo and the crossroads beyond. This entailed the 4th/5th Royal Scots Fusiliers attacking and capturing Alpen. The 6th Cameronians to follow through and push towards the Rhine, whilst the 4th Kings Own Scottish Borderers (KOSBs) were to attack Haus Loo and capture the crossroads beyond. The Scots Guards of the Guards Armoured Division were to capture the ground from Bönninghardt village to the railway line embankment running north out of Alpen. From there Basil and the battalion would attack and capture the Xanten to Rheinberg Road between Menzelen and the crossroads behind Haus Loo, after Haus Loo had been captured by the 4th KOSBs. This plan meant that the 'Wesel pocket' was being attacked on all sides, with the Canadians to the left of Basil and the battalion, the 4th KOSBs to their right, the 6th Cameronians and 4th/5th Royal Scots Fusiliers on their right, with the American forces on the extreme right.

By 2.00pm on the 8th of March it was known that the Americans had met ferocious opposition at Rheinberg and had been fought to a standstill. The 4th/5th Royal Scots Fusiliers attack on Alpen had met strong resistance. The 6th Cameronians attacking around the town had taken very heavy casualties when they strayed into Alpen and were withdrawn. The Canadians were fighting their way into the town of Xanten from the left and were also meeting fanatical opposition.

The 2nd Battalion Scots Guards attack went in at 4.30pm and was successful against stiff opposition, capturing the ground between Bönninghardt and the railway embankment within an hour. For Basil and the battalion, their attack was to follow the Scots Guards attack, so they set off marching down the *Bönninghardter straße* to the airfield by the village, ready to move forward to the start line on the railway embankment the Scots Guards had secured. However, the battalion's attack was cancelled because their right flank was left dangerously exposed by the partial failure of the 4th/5th Royal Scots Fusiliers, and 6th Cameronians attack on Alpen.

Basil and the boys were to spend a cold night exposed on the airfield in hastily dug slit trenches. Shortly after dark, the sky was lit up by an ammunition truck ahead of them – in the Scots Guards position – exploding after a direct hit from one of the many shells targeted at them. In the knowledge that they were to take over that position in the morning, and to launch an attack from there, it is unlikely that they could get much sleep. Once again, the strain involved in steeling themselves for imminent battle and then being delayed must have taken a heavy toll on their nerves.

Overnight the 4th Battalion of the KOSBs took over Alpen woods to allow the 6th Cameronians to launch a night attack on Alpen. This proved to be one of the most disastrous attacks of the campaign. Communications between the Companies and HQ broke down; their Commanding Officer had been temporarily replaced by another who was suffering from malaria and not truly fit for the role. The location of the American 9th Army to their right was unknown, meaning that artillery support could not be offered for fear of inflicting casualties on them. A Company met fierce resistance trying to cross the rail embankment, lost radio contact and withdrew. C Company successfully crossed the rail embankment and advanced to what should have been the boundary of the attacking American 9th Army attacking parallel to them but found no sign of them as they hadn't in fact attacked, again due to communication failures. C Company were therefore left exposed behind the German lines with dawn approaching. The German paratroopers launched a counterattack with armoured support. By 10.00am C Company were overrun. 27 were killed or wounded, the survivors surrendered. B Company launched its own attack on the milk factory just outside Alpen. Having crossed 200 yards of open ground they were pinned down by concentrated fire from a self-propelled gun and paratroopers from the factory. Some were surrounded, taking many casualties. Only D Company reached and held its objective. The attack had eventually secured Alpen but not the milk factory which had a clear line of sight for those inside to direct fire on those who were to later attack Haus Loo.

On a brighter note, the Canadians having taken Xanten were now fighting their way down the Xanten to Rheinberg road and had reached the Alter Rhine water course but that still meant that Basil and the battalion's left flank was still totally exposed.

Whilst the 6th Cameronians attack was fizzling out, early morning on the 9th of March the 4th Battalion of the KOSBs received their orders to attack towards Haus Loo. The men were roused at 3.45am with the information that Alpen had been captured by the 4th/5th Royal Scots Fusiliers and that the 6th Cameronians were pushing on beyond. They could easily see the smoke and flames rising from Alpen. Also worrying news arrived that the railway line had been retaken by the defenders having been previously secured by the Scots Guards. They were to move to their allotted start line near the Alpen to Issum road which they completed under shellfire to attack at 5.00am. It was misty and cold with perhaps 800 yards visibility. By 8.00am the companies, supported with Churchill tanks of the Welsh Guards, were advancing in arrowhead formation through the stubble field towards the railway embankment 1,500 yards away under heavy mortar fire. It soon became clear that the enemy still held the embankment and were firing everything they had at the advancing 4th KOSBs. A self-propelled artillery gun and snipers armed with Spandau machine guns around the milk factory just outside Alpen, that had not been captured by the 6th Cameronians, were also firing mercilessly at them. In less than 90 minutes three of the Welsh Guards tanks had been knocked out by what was thought to be eight 88mm guns sighted around Haus Loo.

At 10.30am civilians were seen streaming towards them from the direction of the railway track, some of them wounded.

It was noon before all the remnants of the 4th KOSBs reached the railway embankment and its protection offered from machine gun fire, but not from the mortars. The attack was stalling badly but at least the enemy had withdrawn from the embankment into the grounds of Haus Loo. The KOSB's heavy losses meant that their objective had now to be reduced to the capture of Haus Loo and not the crossroads beyond. The 4th KOSBs called for artillery support which was not forthcoming. They had to cross over the rail tracks to the other side under a hail of small arms fire from Haus Loo. They were now in full view of the Haus Loo defenders and the snipers in the Alpen milk factory and were hopelessly pinned down under intense Spandau fire, mortars and artillery.

Basil and the battalion waited; the tension and strain must have been unbearable. They were on standby to attack any time after 11.00am. There are only so many times you can check and recheck your equipment. They were not to move until Haus Loo had been captured by the 4th KOSBs so they must have been hoping that any attack involving them would again be cancelled and someone else have to do it. That was not to be. News then came which must have made the officers turn white. They were to attack at 2.30pm even though Haus Loo was still in enemy hands. Their attack would be swept from their right, in enfilade, by artillery and

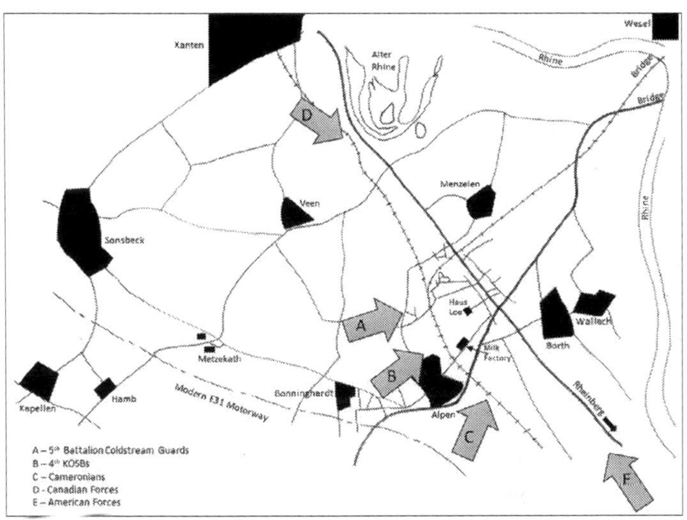

The Wesel Pocket –battle for Haus Loo, 9th March 1945

machine gun fire from the enemy defenders in Haus Loo, in addition to any fire coming from houses in the path of the attack and from the Xanten to Rheinberg Road. This was to make the attack significantly more dangerous. It is unclear whether this information was relayed to Basil and the other men in the companies.

The plan of attack for the battalion was the same as the original plan from the day before. There would be artillery support from nine field guns, three medium guns and two heavy guns. 2 Company would lead on the right nearest to Haus Loo, with 3 Company following behind them. 1 Company would lead on the left of the attack with Basil and 4 Company following up behind them. The Canadians were no closer to occupying the land to their left flank, meaning that 1 Company and Basil's 4 Company would be exposed to enemy fire from their left.

The battalion formed up with the tanks from the 1st Battalion Coldstream Guards as per the training at Opheylissem, one squadron of tanks matched with a company of infantry. At 1.00pm they made their way to the start line behind the railway embankment in the warm afternoon sunshine, the tanks throwing up dust from the unusually dry tracks they traversed along. The enemy luckily had a poor view of them making their way across the flat ground due to a heavy haze caused by smoke from burning houses. This must have masked them from view as they were not shelled. Once behind the railway embankment they started to dig in to gain protection from the expected enemy shells and mortars. There they waited the remaining 30 minutes for the order to attack.

Some of the 4th KOSBs from their pinned down position the other side of the embankment could see an 88mm anti-tank gun sighted at the side of Haus Loo directly looking over the field they were in, firing at them, its shells smashing into the embankment behind them. It was aiming at the 1st Battalion Coldstream Guards' Sherman tanks that were partially hidden 'hull down' behind the embankment awaiting Basil and the battalion's attack.

The Coldstream's artillery support started up at 2.30pm in a crescendo of sound, shaking the ground and prompting the two lead companies to launch the attack as some of the 4th KOSBs looked on from their shell holes just a few yards to the right. As soon as 2 Company appeared over the railway embankment, they were met with murderous fire from the numerous self-propelled artillery guns, mortars and machine guns around Haus Loo, some 700 yards ahead and to their right, and from houses ahead of them. The self-propelled gun sighted at the Alpen milk factory was also ranged on them. The field ahead rapidly becoming cratered with exploding mortars and shells. They immediately started to take casualties.

The lead tank hit a mine as it crossed over the embankment and was knocked out as it crossed the level crossing. The 4th KOSBs, just yards away saw another hit from the 88mm gun sighted beside Haus Loo. In front of the KOSB's eyes the tank burst into flame and to their horror, had to listen to the Sherman's crew being tortured inside the stricken tank as the fire engulfed them. Black billowing smoke and flames emerged from the hatches. The cries for help quickly turned to long drawn-out shrieks of agony until ammunition inside 'cooked off', the explosions silencing them.

The other tanks had to waste time searching for other routes over the embankment. This delay had meant leaving the infantry of 2 Company to take the full force of Haus loo's fire power. They were cut down, all but one of the officers and almost half the company were killed or wounded before they got near their objective, the bodies lying in the green field they were crossing. From their shallow cover the 4th KOSBs could hear the pitiful cries of the wounded calling for stretcher bearers. They watched the next tank race over the rails and down the embankment, stopping close to the still blazing hulk and spraying fire towards Haus Loo.

3 Company were ordered to wait for the tanks to cross the embankment until advancing to benefit from the dubious protection they offered. Artillery positioned in depth, and in Haus Loo, picked off the advancing tanks and continued to pour shells on the railway embankment.

Meanwhile to the left of the attack on and around the railway line, amid the cacophony of sound Basil and 4 Company would have been able to see and hear the tanks alongside 1 Company ahead of them pouring murderous fire on the many German defenders in their path. A self-propelled anti-tank gun was firing from their exposed left flank which destroyed at least one of the tanks before their eyes. 1 Company, with specific orders to bypass as much opposition as possible, advanced rapidly towards their objective leaving pockets of resistance in the nearby houses, gardens, and sheds. Basil, Mansel, George, Paul, and Fred, and all of 4 Company fervidly attacked these with grenades, rifle and machine gun fire. Bitter hand-to-hand fighting with fixed bayonets was needed to displace the highly motivated and fanatical enemy who fought ferociously, defending every inch of ground, in most cases resisting to the last man. As each building was captured, any survivors retreated to the next with their artillery focussing on that lost ground and its new owners. A self-propelled gun ceased firing only when all its crew were dead. Those terrified residents that hadn't been evacuated became inevitable casualties.

The barrage from the artillery behind them was ordered to be extended for a further 15 minutes assisting 1 Company to reach their objective on the Xanten to Rheinberg road and Basil's 4 Company to reach and consolidate their objective on the railway junction behind them. The survivors of 2 Company finally reached their objective on the Xanten to Rheinberg road, whilst 3 Company following behind them significantly observed the enemy pulling out of Haus Loo.

With the aid of smoke canisters, the 4th KOSBs finally attacked and captured the medieval moated area at the rear of Haus Loo, after their C Company had been driven back in a ferocious limited counterattack as far back as the embankment. Their retaking of the lost ground almost caused a friendly fire disaster, only averted by yellow smoke canisters being set off by those already in the moated area. During the attack the defenders fired off all their remaining panzerfausts at point blank range. One severely wounded defender was bayonetted whilst still firing his Spandau machine gun. It was 4.00pm before they cautiously entered a now deserted Haus Loo and reported its capture. This being sometime after Basil and the battalion had captured their objectives and seen the defenders withdrawing from Haus Loo.

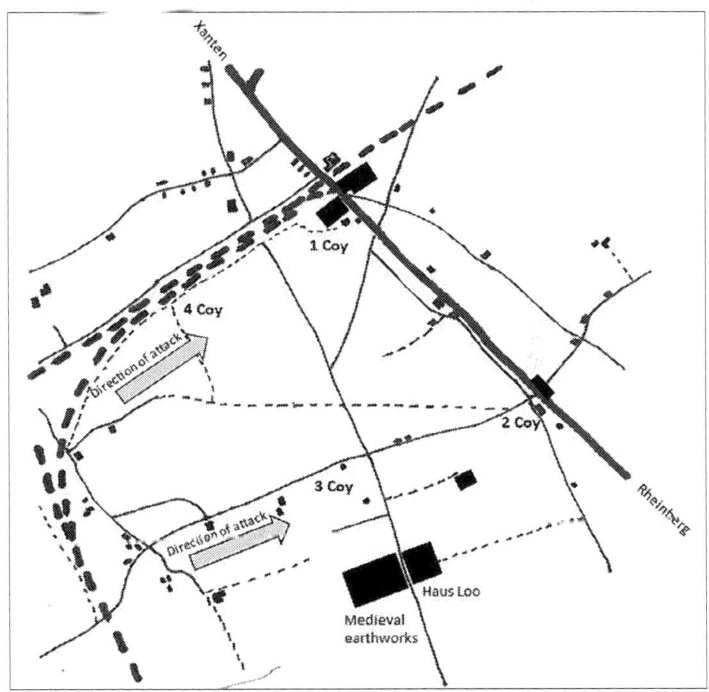

Battalion positions at Haus Loo, 9th March 1945

For Basil and the battalion, consolidating their positions under terrifying heavy nebelwerfer mortar fire and artillery fire was perhaps the hardest part of the whole attack. The enemy were still firing from across the road destroying more of the Coldstream's tanks and self-propelled guns. The shelling and mortaring intensified as the night wore on to the point that it was considered to be the heaviest bombardment they had suffered since landing in Normandy, with all the misery, horror and fear that conjured up. All 'dug in' for all they were worth, expecting a counterattack. It never came and by 11.30pm the battalion was relieved by 5th Battalion Highland Light Infantry who suffered their share of the intense bombardment throughout the night. Basil and the battalion were able then to move wearily back to their previous temporary billets near to Metzekath.

Back in their billets during the night they would have heard two loud muffled explosions. The road and rail bridges at Wesel had been blown up by the retreating defenders. As a direct result of their attack the German position had become untenable as their main supply line had been cut, and they had finally been given permission to withdraw back over the Rhine. In the morning when it became clear just what they had achieved, the boys must have felt elated. They knew they had done a great job. They would have believed that they were the best, *second to none* as per the battalion motto. Probably most of all, they were delighted to be alive after the terrifying fighting they had been at the forefront of over the past few weeks.

The 4th KOSBs weren't so lucky, they had to dig in for the night around the moated area and the house, preparing for the counterattack that never came. In the morning the 7th and 9th Royal Scots Fusiliers passed through them towards the Rhine supported by Cromwell tanks and an artillery barrage. Once the Royal Scots Fusiliers had passed through and out of sight, they were able to survey their surroundings in daylight. Several dead defenders lay scattered around the moated area and the shattered orchard. Multiple dead and wounded 4th KOSBs lay in the field between Haus Loo and the railway embankment. They found the cattle sheds at the rear of the house that surrounded a courtyard to be in a pitiful state. The roofs had multiple hits from mortar and shell fire which has cascaded inside onto the horses and cattle. The walls punctured by artillery and tank fire. Many of the animals were wounded and others terrified. All the cows were suffering from the need for milking. The 4th KOSBs took it on themselves to destroy those in the worst condition. These were buried nearby in the field with the help of surviving local civilians and liberated slave workers. The rear of the house had received a direct hit that penetrated the rear wall of one of the bedrooms. On entering the house they were confronted with damaged plaster, broken glass and smashed furniture. The beautiful home had been looted. Every room had drawers pulled out, personal papers, clothes and photographs scattered about ankle deep. At the front of the house one or two dead defenders were scattered along with their equipment. At the side of the house facing the field over which the Coldstreams had attacked, empty shell cases from the anti-tank gun installed there lay scattered about. It remained for the 4th KOSBs to bury their dead in the open field near the house. They watched as whining carriers busied across the field collecting the bodies and equipment of the fallen Coldstreams, mostly from the battalion's 2 Company.

B company of the 4th KOSBs moved into the house to set up their HQ. One of the B Company officers, Peter White, entered the cellar late in the evening to find the officer commanding C Company having already set up his HQ there. Lieutenant Peter White described the cellar as being partitioned off with blankets hung up as curtains. The floor covered with straw. In one corner a family of German men women and children were trying to prepare food by the light of a candle.

The 4th KOSBs remained at Haus Loo for 3 days, enduring the thunderous noise of the 25-pounder artillery unit that set up around the building early on the morning of the 11th of March, firing ear bursting salvos towards the Rhine and beyond. They eventually moved out at 9.00pm on the 12th of March via Alpen to Marienbaum.

18

Counting the cost

The family that Lieutenant Peter White of the 4th KOSBs saw in the cellar of Haus Loo preparing food by candle light was the Bremer family who were the long term residents of Haus Loo. One of the children was 13-year-old Erika Bremer. Erika's first-hand account relayed to me and interpreted in March 2022 is as follows:

"Earlier in the war we were sent Russian prisoners as helpers on the farm. On one occasion they were making fried potatoes and one of them threw the plate of food onto the table. My father complained about their attitude, and they were taken away. They were replaced with Polish prisoners as helpers. They were very nice people.

At some point before the fighting passed over us German officers arrived and stayed in the house. They seemed to have a lot of lady visitors!

The Rheinberg-Xanten railway line was violently attacked from the air. The daughter of the neighbours was killed. We were not evacuated because our house was too far away from the other houses, and no one informed us. The neighbours had all left and we were the only ones left behind.

There was an anti-aircraft gun to the right of Haus Loo but I didn't see any other guns. Father kept telling the German soldiers to give up the house and get to safety, but they were forbidden to do so. Haus Loo was targeted from the direction of the Bönninghardt Ridge and as the front grew closer we all moved into the cellar. The Polish prisoners wanted to go into the cellar with us but the German soldiers forbade it and at some point they were gone. We lived in all four basement rooms for about a week. If there was an attack on the house, we had to go to the only room without windows as father was afraid that grenades would be thrown through the windows. The disadvantage of this was that this room was directly opposite the stairs. It could have been that the soldiers would shoot through the door when they went into the cellar. It wasn't so cold in the cellar because we had an oven for cooking that gave off heat. We heard the tanks approaching and could hear the milk cows screaming, urgently needing to be milked. The horses were completely distraught by the attacks. We could not help the animals because we had to stay safe. My father was injured in the leg by a shell when trying to do so. The British took him to a hospital. However, we did not know where exactly he was for a few days. The local priest helped us to search. Until late in life, he limped as a result of the injury.

A British soldier wanted to steal a chicken from the chicken coop and my brother tried to stop him. During the dispute, the British soldier accidentally dropped a hand grenade. My brother was killed instantly and the soldier's heel was blown off. My brother was buried in the roundel in front of the house but later moved to the Alpen cemetery. The chicken coop was a small building to the left of the house. That aside, the British or Scots, I don't know which, treated me well and were very nice.

The window at the top left of the side of the courtyard was torn out by a shell and there was a big hole in the wall. When the war was over, the house was looted. There were many disoriented people on the road (former prisoners of war, soldiers, etc.) looking for food and valuables. My father was still in the hospital at that time and mother and I were alone in the house. As it was too unsafe for us there, we first cycled to Alpen, but there were no more people there. Then we went on to Issum to a cousin's house and stayed for three weeks. My other brother had been drafted into the Wehrmacht in the last days of the war and no one knew where exactly he was. Some time after the end of the war, the locals looked for their animals in the neighbourhood. This often led to quarrels, as everyone claimed it was their animal. The one who was more energetic was often able to get his way."

The civilians the 4th KOSBs saw coming towards them over the railway tracks may well have been the Polish prisoners (slave workers) from Haus Loo. Their lodgings were at the rear of the house by the cattle barns and would have been in grave danger from the shelling. Its logical that they would have made their way to the British lines. Alternatively, they may have been the ones who assisted in burying the dead livestock.

The 4th KOSBs had accrued a reputation for 'relieving' the farms they passed through of virtually anything edible – eggs, milk, chickens etc. On this occasion their apparent lust for their craft proved shamefully fatal for Erika's brother.

Mercifully 13 year old Erica was saved the awful sights of the dead and injured livestock. By the time she emerged from the cellar these, and the human carnage littering the battlefield around the house had mostly been cleared. The family paid a high price for living in the house that was ultimately the scene of the last desperate stand made by German forces before their forced retreat across the Rhine, thus drawing to a close the bitter bloody contest for the Rhineland.

The battle for Haus Loo had been won at a fearsome cost. 13 of the 5th Battalion Coldstream Guardsmen lay dead and a further 38 wounded. The 1st Battalion Coldstream lost several destroyed tanks and their crews. Of the 52nd Lowland Division, the 4th KOSBs alone sustained 80 casualties, most of them fatal. The 6th Cameronians disastrously lost 4 officers and 157 men killed, wounded or captured. The German defenders were from the elite 22 Parachute Regiment, of the 7th Parachute Division and again it is unclear how many of their number were killed or wounded. The total number of prisoners of war taken by Basil's battalion was 128 with many more taken by the 52nd Lowland Division. One unlucky prisoner inadvertently drove into 1 Company's position after dark with a ration lorry.

There were many significant and celebrated moments during WW2 that turned the course of the war that are indelibly stamped in history and known to most people. The great victories of the 'Battle of Britain', 'D-Day', and the 'Battle of the Bulge' are amongst the best known examples. Even dramatic failures like 'Dunkirk' and 'Arnhem' are known by most. The common theme is that they are all depicted in blockbuster movies or have received large amounts of publicity over the years. The decisive battle for Haus Loo, that had forced Hitler to withdraw his forces back across the Rhine was a significant victory that concluded the battle of the Rhineland. Like many other WW2 battles, such as the battles in Normandy and the River Scheldt in Holland, it has been largely quietly forgotten and unknown of today except by keen war historians. This being despite the fact that it was fought in the worst possible weather conditions, pushed human endurance to the limit, and featured some of the most ferocious fighting and intense shellfire of the war. The Germans were after all fighting fanatically and bravely for their homeland. However, back in March 1945 Basil, George, Mansel, Paul and Fred, and all of the battalion were credited with being the 'straw that broke the camel's back'. This was their moment in history! Their capture of the Xanten to Rheinberg road had forced the German withdrawal from Haus Loo and denied the 4th KOSBs from having that credit. Once the euphoria had died down, they were probably just content to know that they were to move back to safe, warm billets in Mook near Nijmegen. For them for a while at least the fighting was over. Time to recover their shattered nerves. Time for the discipline of the Coldstream Guards to knock them back into a fully fit fighting unit. Time for thoughts to turn to home.

19

The anxiety at home

Back home the 'blackout' was tedious. Cumnor had three Air Raid Precaution Marshalls who were always patrolling and looking for chinks of light coming from house windows. On one occasion there was a sharp rap on the door and shouting outside. 'Put that light out!' They had left the back window and curtain open. On another, late one evening, when almost everyone was in bed, an aircraft flew at rooftop height over the house as a warning. The pilot could see the house wasn't in 'blackout'. It made the whole house shake and frightened the living daylights out of all of them. The culprit was Mary, who had been sitting in the kitchen with a mirror propped up against the white enamel bread bin, doing her make-up and hair. She had forgotten to draw the curtains.

Apart from the 'blackout', and of course the rationing, the civilian population went about their business as if it were peacetime. London and other major cities were still the targets for the V1 and V2 attacks and the papers were always carrying stories of these attacks but life in Cumnor couldn't have been more remote from the war raging in Europe and in the far east.

In early March the newspaper and radio headlines were filled with the news that the Americans had famously, and very luckily, managed to secure the undamaged Ludendorff bridge over the Rhine at Remagen and were already advancing towards Cologne and Bonn south of the Rhineland. The British and Canadian gargantuan struggles in the Rhineland had largely taken a back seat in the newspapers to these American successes. On the 23rd of March however, the newspapers lit up with stories on the progress of the war in the Rhineland. The bridges at Wesel had been blown up and the last of the German forces had retreated across the Rhine. British and Canadian troops had secured a great victory.

The battle Basil and the boys had just fought at Haus Loo had been witnessed and described by several war correspondents. Censorship had just been lifted on the war, so articles describing the attack appeared in the national dailies for the first time naming the regiment involved. 'The Times' newspaper reported the attack as its lead article on the 23rd of March, in typical exuberant, eloquent style. It was entitled 'The Guards in Action'. The reporter had been accompanying the 1st Battalion Coldstream Guards in their Sherman tanks and was to report on their prowess in the attack, but an altercation with one of the officers just prior to it changed the target of his report to Basil and the battalion. He called it a *heroic episode of supreme daring in one of the hardest fought battles of the war*'. In describing the attack, he complemented the battalion as being '*a fine example of disciplined valour, having advanced over 1,000 yards of bullet swept open ground under a hail of fire from front and flanks against furious resistance, clearing buildings room by room*. Within the article, a sergeant in one of the supporting tanks commented that for the first time he had to close his turret due to the intensity of the artillery and small arms fire and was in awe of the bravery of the battalion's charge. The article continues with describing the German parachutists as *'being of the fiercest fanatical troops in their army, indoctrinated with racial myths and pagan ideologies designed to turn them into effective killing machines'*. In comparison to this the great traditions of the Coldstream Guards that *'inspire steadiness and imperturbability that can turn the fortunes of an attack against hardcore resistance, retreat, or disaster'* are exulted. He even likened the battalion to the elite Roman legion known as the *'Triarii'* whose main function was to be used as a decisive force in a battle. Aside from the heroic description of the attack it leads on to examine the stark difference between the training of the Coldstream Guards and the German parachutists, describing the latter as being *'arrogant, dehumanised, and made unsuitable for citizenship'*, whereas the Coldstream Guards were *'nurtured on drill, discipline, and the honour and duty of a guardsman'*. It is asserted that these qualities together with their *'courage, efficiency, good behaviour, and friendliness'* outmatched the *'chosen product of a killer caste'*.

This was the first time that Lillian would have known anything about where Basil was. All she could have known was that he was somewhere oversees with the Coldstream Guards. She would have been sending letters to him but Basil, like all those on 'active service' would have only been able to send small brown postcards back saying nothing more than they were well and had received the letter. Lillian was not someone who would have read 'The Times' newspaper but the Walkers and the Blackwells she cleaned for almost certainly would have done and would have brought the article to her attention. This would have been a bombshell for her. Not knowing where Basil was minimised her worries, and she had always been a worrier. Out of sight is out of mind as the saying goes. She would now have known that Basil was in the thick of the action and her anxiety must have been pushed through the roof at this news.

The usual gathering around the old radio in the kitchen to hear the BBC six o'clock news would have taken on a new intensity. 'Woodbines' and immersing herself in hard work helped, but she had also been communicating by letter with Mansel's mother. This must have given her strength; two worried mothers together offering mutual support and friendship. The friendship extended to Mansel's mother inviting her over for the day to the farm at Weston on the Green. Lillian, Iris and Vera in their best dresses took the bus to Gloucester Green bus terminal at Oxford. There they caught the bus to Weston on the Green and spent the day on the farm. They had a roast dinner and met Mansel's father, elder brother, and twin brother who was able to remain working as Mansel had gone to war in his place. Mansel's son Neil, explained to me that

"Father was one of three sons, the story goes that his older brother was reserved occupation. When one of the farm workers was called up, he was able to stay on the farm. Then came father's call-up being older than his twin brother, but he failed his medical, having a cold at the time. His twin brother then failed his

medical, flat feet, I think! Dad was called back in and off he went for training. I think that was April 1944. He was 18 years old in December 1943."

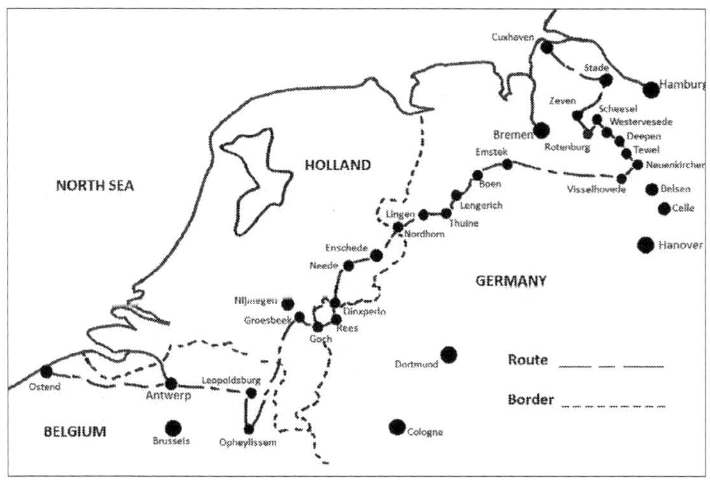

Basil's route from Ostend to Cuxhaven

20

Crossing the Rhine

Basil had arrived in Mook near Nijmegen, Holland on the 12th of March 1945 in the early evening looking forward to a well-earned rest. The weather had improved dramatically, and flowers were blooming in the old war-torn battlefields. Nijmegen and Mook were slowly returning to a form of normality, having been liberated since September. Along with the American gliders, a few of the Horsa gliders that Lillian, Iris and Vera had seen passing low over the house on that misty Sunday morning were still lying in the fields around Nijmegen where they landed, some intact, some just mangled skeletons. Grasses growing around and through them. Basil and the boys must have slept well in the safest environment they had been in for some time. They could look forward to the cinema and entertainment evenings, trips into Brussels and surrounding welcoming towns and villages. There would be mobile baths and shaves and new kit to be issued, re-enforcements to be inducted, and it wouldn't be long before the discipline of the

Coldstreams kicked in with the familiar polishing, bulling, and inspections.

It seems incredible but within four days of arriving, Basil and the boys of 4 Company were whisked off for four days to the residence of the provisional governor of North Brabant, in Eindhoven, during the stay there of the Dutch Queen Wilhelmina. They had to parade on several occasions for her inspection, with all the pomp that went with such a peacetime guard's role. They must have been seething over this foolhardy use of their time. It must have seemed inconceivable that a few days before, they had been through hell and were now parading with pressed uniforms and bulled boots. I wonder what Queen Wilhelmina saw in Basil's eyes when she inspected him. He stood ramrod straight, in battledress and green beret sporting a shined Coldstream star, Lee Enfield sloped over his left shoulder and bayonet fixed. Did he still have that thousand-yard stare that it is said that combat troops have when they have just come out of a long period of intense fighting?[1]

Whilst Basil and the boys were compelled to complete this distinctly unwarlike activity, a lot had been going on. The crossing of the Rhine commenced on the 24th of March, codenamed Operation Plunder. It involved amphibious landings at Rees, Wesel, and south of Wesel. It was co-ordinated with airborne landings east of the river codenamed Operation Varsity.

The squadrons of C47 Dakotas, Iris had seen struggling to clear the roof of the house were now being used as part of the largest airborne assault in one day, in one location, in history. From his location in Mook, at 10.00am, Basil and every other soldier and civilian alike would have been looking skyward to the biggest aerial phenomenon they would ever see. The bombardment that had been rumbling away had stopped and replaced by the distant deep drone of aircraft. At low altitude, wave after wave of C47 Dakotas, in perfect formation roared overhead. Towards the rear of the air armada were the towed gliders. The sky train stretched nearly 200 miles and took over 2½ hours to pass them. They were escorted by over 600 British and American fighter planes above them. Nearly 18,000 airborne troops landed in the drop zone just across the Rhine at Wesel which was only 5 miles deep and 6 miles wide. By the following morning, and after heavy fighting, a sizable bridgehead was established.

The battalion were unable to cross as a mixed unit with the 1st Battalion tanks until a bridge had been built strong enough to take the heavy tanks across. On the 28th of March they left Mook and travelled in darkness to a hill just outside the town of Uedem. There they joined up with the 1st Battalion tanks and waited their turn to cross the river. They were in the area of a previous battle, with ruined houses and the ground still scattered with land mines. 2 Company strayed into a minefield resulting in five casualties.

They finally crossed the Rhine over a floating pontoon bridge predictably named 'London Bridge' at around 3pm on Good Friday, the 30th of March near the now destroyed town of Rees. Once across the river they headed through German territory for the town of Dinxperloo on the German, Dutch border, where they halted for the night.

This was another triumphant moment for Basil and the boys. It is not hard to imagine them crossing the slightly wobbly pontoon bridge in their armoured carriers with the dark fast moving waters of the mighty Rhine just beneath them, tanks in front and behind. It was a dull damp overcast day, but they must have felt elated, lost in the magnitude of the moment, of pride in themselves, and a refreshed buoyant confidence. This was the prize for their gallant hard-fought actions at Müll, Buchholt, Metzekath and Haus Loo that finally pushed the Germans back over the Rhine. They were now part of the next significant moment in the war.

The Guards Armoured Division, of which Basil and the battalion were a part of, had been given the job of breaking out of the bridgehead that had cost so many lives to secure. They were to start off leading their army group (XXX Corps) northeast towards Bremen and Hamburg in north Germany. The route would first take them north into Holland with the first objective being to seize and cross the bridge over the Twente Canal at the Dutch town of Enschede. They were to avoid any opposition where possible in the race to the bridge which was known to be strongly held.

The following day they started the break-out from the bridgehead. Basil and 4 Company, paired with the tanks from 2 Squadron of the 1st Battalion, were to lead the entire group. Under a cloudy sky they advanced through the village of Lichtenvoorde which was cleared of some opposition. They then branched left via Zieuwent village to Borculo, which was found to be held by the Germans, so turned right to Beltrum, and left towards the village of Neede. As they passed through a wooded area the lead tanks were fired on from houses to the right side of them. They returned fire, setting the houses ablaze. Basil and 4 Company were sent in to 'mop up' and had a vicious firefight as they entered and cleared the houses, taking 56 Prisoners of War and leaving many dead defenders.

They were then halted just outside Neede, close to a concrete factory, when a tank and an armoured car were knocked out due to the Germans making a stand there. They remained the night outside Neede with Basil and 4 Company posted astride the main road to Borculo village. During the night there were several small nerve shattering encounters with the enemy trying to infiltrate their lines, resulting in more prisoners of war taken. By the morning of the 1st of April, the Germans had pulled out and the way was clear for 4 Company with 2 Squadron's tanks to lead the way towards the Twente Canal bridge at Enschede. Halfway there, at 08.00am, as they entered the village of Beckum they met with light opposition, taking another 110 prisoners of war.

All along the route there were desperate groups of refugees, men, women, and children struggling with their bundles of belongings, freed from captivity or fleeing from the fighting. Some managed a smile through drawn pale faces. Most looked overcome with despair or shock from whatever they had endured, walking in an apparent trance-like state devoid of expression, only the youngsters managed a wave .

At 09.15am due to a slight navigational error, the lead tanks of 2 Squadron came across the canal unexpectedly around a quarter of a mile away from the bridge which was over to their left. A number of Germans could be seen on the bridge. All hell broke loose as they raced away from Basil and 4 Company and rushed the bridge along the concrete road beside the canal bank, machine gunning the bridge to clear the Germans off, and firing shells and rockets at the far bank which was held by several 88mm German artillery guns and supporting infantry. Three of the tanks got across just as the bridge was blown up. Six of the tanks were knocked out by the 88mm artillery during this effective ambush in front of Basil and the boy's eyes. Some of the surviving crew members stripped and swam back across the river.

The Canal comes to an end not far east of the blown-up bridge within Enschede town itself, so plans were quickly made to circumvent the Canal. 1 Company with 1 Squadron tanks were sent to get around the end of the canal where they met up with the sole survivor of the 2 squadron tanks that had heroically fought its way along the far bank. The crew reported strong enemy forces so 1 company were ordered to hold the position whilst plans were made to form a bridgehead into the town involving the entire battalion. Once the bridgehead was formed, the Germans pulled out of the town centre leaving some strong opposition in the west by the canal. The enemy still controlled the north route out of the town so other elements of the Guards Armoured Division passed through the battalion to take them on.

By 5.30 pm the firing had almost stopped and suddenly Basil, Mansel, George, Paul, and Fred, and the whole of the battalion found themselves swamped by grateful residents who appeared jubilantly in the streets. Basil and the boys had liberated the starving population of Enschede from almost six long years of Nazi oppression. The damp and miserable weather went unnoticed as their enthusiasm spilled over into adulation for the men of the Coldstream Guards.

Since the latter part of 1944 the Germans had pillaged most of Holland's food and heating supplies leaving the population in a desperate state. There is film footage of the liberation available on the internet showing these jubilant scenes, of the people in their best Sunday clothes running to get a better view of their liberators, women with ribbons in their hair, men with pointed party hats, people riding on the tanks and carriers waving wildly. It was Easter Sunday. The boys in the tanks, carriers, and those on foot were being presented with their precious fruit, cakes and flowers. That was all that was available for them to offer.

The mood amongst the battalion would have been at an all-time high as they could sense that the war was in its final stages, but this welcome must have filled them with pride. To have felt the joy of that day must have been incredible; lasting memories were forged.[2]

This was in stark contrast to the scenes they had encountered with the pitiful German residents of the towns they had passed through, where they were surviving in the ruins of the buildings, peering out of glassless windows with pale gaunt faces. Those on the wayside wearing expressionless masks to cover their feelings. 'Hitler no good!' Was the common response if spoken to. Very few showed any hostility, some tried not to notice the invaders at all.

Whilst all the newspapers and BBC radio were full of the news of the Rhine Crossings, on the 27th of March 1945, a V2 Rocket landed between Court Road and Kynaston Road, Orpington, Kent and killed one person. Two days later a V1 Flying Bomb, commonly known as a 'Doodlebug', fell out of the sky and landed in a field close to a sewage farm at Woolmer Green, Hertfordshire. There were no casualties. Though nobody realised at the time, these two bombs would prove to be the last of Hitler's 'vengeance' weapons to land in Britain during the War. Their launch sites had finally been pushed out of range by the advances into Germany and Holland that Basil and thousands of allied troops had worked so hard to achieve.

Notes

1   The Imperial War Museum have a photograph of Queen Wilhelmina inspecting 4 Company – Ref no. BU1927
2   Every year the residents of Enschede still celebrate the liberation with parades of brass bands, wartime army vehicles, decorated floats and a carnival atmosphere. Near the canal bridge, where they died, is a memorial to the tank crews that were first across the bridge. The Imperial War Museum have a photograph of the Guards Armoured Division entering Enschede – Ref no. BU2947 and others

21

North-west Germany

Basil and the battalion stayed the night in Enschede before finally moving out to more jubilant waving, leaving follow-up troops to deal with the six hospitals they had found full of around 5,000 German wounded. This time other elements of the Guards Armoured Division took the lead. They headed through Oldenzaal towards the German border at Nordhorn which proved to be strongly defended. The battalion stopped in woods just outside Denekamp on the Dutch side of the border for the night whilst the leaders of the Guards Armoured Division battled their way through and bridged the three canals that had their bridges blown up on the route.

On the following dull and miserable morning, the battalion emerged from their uncomfortable damp slit trenches they had dug the night before. The air thick with the smell of petrol and hex fires brewing tea. They soon moved off in their TCLs to join the long line of tanks and other vehicles that formed their Coldstream Battle

Group. Together they crossed the German frontier, then through Nordhorn towards the town of Lingen. Between them and Lingen was the river Ems and a little further on, the large Dortmund-Ems Canal, the target of many Bomber Command raids. The battalion halted and formed a protective front line with 4 Company located in the village of Nordlohne, whilst a report of an un-blown bridge was checked out. One of Basil's commanders, Captain Ian Liddell, had previously been promoted to company commander of 3 Company. He led an attack on the bridge and single handedly diffused bombs set to explode. He then led his company across to capture the bridge. He won a Victoria Cross for his bravery.

Wednesday the 4th of April saw 2 and 3 Companies in action clearing the land between the river Ems and the canal. They attacked a large army barracks taking 142 prisoners of war. Other elements of the Division captured Lingen, enabling the battalion to eventually move off towards Bremen two days later. The Germans put up an extraordinarily strong defence at Ramsel, and again at Thuine, where Typhoon fighter bombers were called in to attack the defenders. These Hawker Typhoons, battling against the poor weather and occasional rainstorms, each delivered their eight rockets in their signature shallow dive. This is the first time the war diary mentions Typhoon rocket attacks actually taking place in support of the battalion's engagements, although they had been in use since D-Day in a 'cab rank' system whereby ground troops could request their services and expect an attack within about 20 minutes. Throughout Operation Veritable in February and early March the weather had been so bad that they were unable to provide such support.

In the assault of Haus Loo, again they had been unable to provide support as the German anti-aircraft firepower was so concentrated around the Wesel pocket that it was too costly for them to perform their low level attacks. I can imagine Basil looking up at the aerial attacks coming in on the Thuine defenders, the Typhoons in their shallow dives, the puff of smoke and belching sound as the rockets were released, and the smoke trails of the rockets as they thundered towards their ground targets. The aircraft disappearing from view behind trees before pulling up in a hard climb on full throttle. The effect must have been devastating for the defenders and Thuine was captured when the tanks advanced immediately after the rocket attack.

Just outside Thuine they liberated a large convent being used as a prisoner of war camp. It contained 350 prisoners of war, mainly Poles, Czechs, Yugoslavs, and French. Also held captive were six Irish Guardsmen who had been captured recently when their tank had been destroyed near Enschede. They were marched back into Germany where they were imprisoned in the convent. They must have been overjoyed to be liberated by Basil and the boys but their joy was short-lived. They had been registered as prisoners of war, so the war was over for them, or so they thought. However, they were ordered to continue the advance and allocated a new tank. Their protestations led them to be placed under arrest. The fact that they were actually registered as prisoners of war saved them from Court Marshal. The liberation of the prisoners was filmed and shown at the cinemas back home on 'British Movietone News'. The short film footage can be found on 'You Tube' entitled 'In the wake of the Hun'.

The advance moved on to attack the town of Lengerich, which held out against attacks from various elements of the Guards Armoured Division. When it fell, a further 111 prisoners of war were captured. The advance continued towards the small town of Berge, an important communications centre for the Germans with large numbers of defenders known to be there waiting. On the route, roadblocks were encountered at every village, which were booby trapped, and stubbornly defended. Again, Typhoons attacked with rockets, this time under much more favourable conditions of bright sunlight and clear skies, followed up with artillery and mortar fire. The tanks attacked from the south but two were soon ablaze, knocked out by panzerfausts fired at close range from windows of the houses so the others had to pull back as the road was blocked. The war diary merely states:

'No. 4 Company cleared from South to North. The first half was carried out without undue difficulty but in the North-East corner a pocket of enemy held out most stubbornly and was only cleared up after several attempts.'

For Basil and the boys this must have been yet another terrifying brutal experience. This attack involved fighting their way down the smoke filled main street, entering and clearing each burning house as they came to them, mostly via the rear gardens with the tanks firing in support down the main street. As per their well-practiced technique, the door was kicked open, grenades thrown in, followed by a burst of machine gun as they entered each room. The surviving stunned defenders were from the 7th Parachute

Division who followed their orders and fought bravely to the last man, resulting in drawn out bitter firefights and hand to hand fighting. Once Basil and 4 Company had cleared to the north end of the main street, 1 Company attacked from east to west. 107 prisoners of war were eventually taken and at least 100 Germans killed. Amazingly only two guardsmen were killed but several more were wounded. By the end of the battle practically every house was on fire.

22

The attack on Boën

The next objective for the battalion was to be the crossing of the River Haze near the village of Boën. Between Berge and Boën were several rivers, all having had the bridges over them destroyed by the retreating Germans. The battalion had to wait outside Berge for other elements of the Guards Armoured Division to force crossings, and for temporary bridges to be built. At least the weather had remained fine.

Finally at 0500 am on Wednesday the 11th of April the battalion were driven in TCLs close to the village of Herbergen, losing one vehicle along the way to a land mine. They formed up along the Buhenenbach Canal and stopped for an early breakfast. The whole battalion then advanced tentatively on foot over the three miles of flat meadows towards the Haze riverbank, the rifle companies in open order with 2 Company leading. They were followed by a troop of 1st Battalion Sherman tanks intent on rushing the bridge if the chance arose. A heavy grey morning mist mercifully shrouded their passage from hidden observers across the river. Felled tree trunks had been strewn on the approach road to the bridge which proved no major obstacle to the tanks and luckily not booby trapped. The rising sun quickly dispersed the mist revealing their unexpected proximity to the riverbank and an already blown up bridge. The enemy were dug in on the far bank and presented a strong defence with small arms fire as soon as they sighted the advancing guardsmen, who at this point were no more than 50 yards away. This caused them to rapidly find very limited cover and return fire, taking casualties as they did so.

The hastily drawn up plan was to wait until dark to force a crossing using assault boats at the most favourable point a short distance to their right where there were some trees to provide cover. 2 Company got the short straw. It was very clear that to force a crossing would mean a very costly affair as artillery support was not possible due to the close proximity of the combatants, the river being no more than 30 yards wide. Amazingly, whilst plans were fervently being made, an escaped French prisoner of war appeared and informed them of an intact bridge two miles further along the bank to their right.

4 Company were sent to investigate, so Basil, Mansel, George, Paul and Fred found themselves clambering onto the backs of the 1st Battalion Sherman tanks, hanging on for dear life and pressing themselves precariously against the turret trying to minimise their profile. The procession of tanks with the rest of 4 Company hanging on formed a convoy as they lurched their way along the undulating rough track through the river meadows, and fresh undamaged farmland. They raced away from the rest of the battalion still pinned down on the riverbank cowering from the intense incoming fire.

The cacophony of sound grew fainter, and finally masked by the clattering of the tracks and exhaust roar from the Shermans. Their thoughts must have been initially of relief having escaped from a very dangerous situation, but their trepidation must have grown as they progressed along the track and saw the bridge they were looking for come into view. That would have sparked their concerns as every bridge they had come across in their advance had either been already blown up or heavily defended. The bridge was far from what was expected, it was merely a small wooden bridge incapable of supporting the tanks and was clearly defended as they immediately came under small arms fire from the opposite bank. This prompted a rapid dismount and struggle to find cover behind the tanks and nearby ditches.

The bridge had been blown but a few planks still remained, making a crossing on foot in single file possible. A fire plan was quickly agreed with the troop of tanks who proceeded to pound the enemy positions on the other side of the river with high explosive shells. Basil and all of 4 Company immediately attacked, in broad daylight. Although under withering fire from about 150 defenders on the opposite bank doing their utmost to cut them down, they stormed the bridge, doubled over against the hail of bullets. They were immediately taking casualties but pressed on across the bridge and into the sparse cover. The speed of the attack made the panic stricken defenders run for cover in the hamlet of Bokah about 500 yards to the north, whilst Basil and 4 Company careered after them and into the buildings. The bloody firefight resulted in all the defenders being killed or captured but at a cost of several of Basil's comrades being killed or wounded.

The other three companies followed, and a bridgehead secured and protected by the firepower of the tanks left on the other side of the river. Distant self-propelled guns soon got the range of the wooden bridge and targeted accurate shellfire on 2 Company tasked with securing it.

This action was an incredibly brave act by all of 4 Company. The company commander, Captain Hamilton won a Military Cross for this action, and as per the charge at Metzekath, Basil, Mansel, George, Paul, and Fred, and all of the company were right with him, earning their share of this moment.[1]

The capture of the wooden bridge opened up the opportunity for an attack to capture Boën and the north bank of the river Haze to gain a bridgehead around the blown road bridge. This would enable a temporary Bailey bridge to be rapidly constructed to carry the tanks across and through Boën. The new plan thus involved an attack on the village together with an attack on the defenders on the river bank. The war diary states:

1745 Hours The Battalion was in position with the right No. 1 Company, left 3 Company, and behind them right 4 Company and left 2 Company.

The whole battalion advanced on foot from Bokah, in the hot sunshine, the two miles back along the riverbank through the dense Buren Tannen fir wood, dealing with scattered defenders and accurate shellfire enroute. They fought their way to the edge of the wood which was to be the start line of their next attack on Boën village itself.

At 6.30pm, the pre-arranged artillery provided by two

field regiments, two medium regiments and the heavy mortar platoon, opened up from across the river onto the quaint village as the whole battalion attacked across the open ground between the wood and their target. Ahead of them they could see the shells crashing home into the buildings causing large grey clouds of smoke and fire, laced with debris. They could hear the roar of their passage like freight trains passing overhead and feel the percussion as they struck. The cacophony of sound must have stunned their senses, but the attack drove on towards the houses. The shocked defenders steadfastly returned considerable small arms fire from the windows of the blasted and smoking ruins, inflicting more casualties. The men in the rifle companies crashed into the buildings and took on the defenders with grenades and hand to hand ferocious fighting. The defenders in many of the houses choosing to fight to the end. Small fire fights and sniping went on for several hours, until dusk finally saw the wrecked and reeking village captured.

The defenders with their backs to the riverbank also courageously held their ground and were only dealt with after severe intense fighting of the worst kind. By 8pm it was all over and the Royal Engineers were able to start building the Bailey bridge. The battalion were supplied by ferries as the route over the wooden bridge was no longer guarded and was only suitable for foot traffic.

Many of the defenders were killed as they bravely held their positions to the end. 192 prisoners were finally taken. The cost in lives to the battalion in securing the river Haze crossing was 17 dead, 4 of them from 4 Company including lance sergeant Clitheroe who had won a military medal at Müll on the Siegfried Line. 4 Company lost 7 of the 51 wounded.

The attack on Boën proved to be a much larger engagement than any other encountered since crossing the Rhine. The Brussels Sprout newsletter on Saturday the 14th of April 1945 printed an account of the progress made from the Ems River crossing to the capture of Boën.[1]

The next day Basil and the battalion watched the 5th Brigade lead the advance whilst they remained to mourn and bury their dead. Basil would have likely known all of the 4 Company dead and wounded, especially lance sergeant Clitheroe.

On Friday the 13th of April they once again married up with the 1st Battalion tanks and led the advance towards the town of Emstek where they were to have a few days much needed rest.

On route they found the village of Lusche to be defended. 3 Company and supporting tanks were about to attack when a friendly fire incident happened, whereby allied aircraft dropped bombs on the attacking column. Despite the incident the attack went in, and the enemy fled without further resistance. This was the third time that Basil and the boys had witnessed friendly fire incidents. Having your own aircraft accidentally attacking must have been very unnerving to already strained nerves. They had been in constant danger and fought multiple terrifying engagements for over two weeks since crossing the Rhine.

The BBC news had been reporting that all resistance in Germany had virtually ceased. It certainly wouldn't have seemed like that to Basil and the battalion. Their morale had been severely dented since the heady liberation of Enschede. Other forces had found the opposition far easier than they had, hence the news reports. Their experience was that of finding roads rendered impassable by huge craters, roadblocks, stubbornly and skilfully defended villages, blown bridges, and constant long waits for temporary bridges to be built to continue the advance. All had been capably planned by the enemy to inflict casualties again and again. Their losses had been steadily mounting from the series of small but costly engagements and then the full-scale battle at Boën. They were physically and mentally exhausted by the time they settled at Emstek on the 14th of April. They had been facing one of the most organised, resourced and expertly led fighting units of the war, the 1st Parachute Army. Despite heavy losses their fighting spirit never diminished.

Throughout the fighting in the Rhineland during Operation Veritable, and whilst passing through Rees to Dinxperloo, the battalion had been on German soil. The artillery fire and bombing, in addition to the extensive flooding had caused almost total devastation to the villages and towns. Most of the population had been evacuated and those remaining so stunned as to be almost oblivious to their invaders, so there had been little contact with German civilians. Most nights had been spent in slit trenches, away from buildings, that were 'dug in' immediately when they halted for the night. Once they had crossed the border back into Germany, they found that the local population had remained in their homes in areas where the German defenders had decided not to stand and fight. This led to the army order forbidding them to fraternise with the locals and consider them as hostile. Guardsmen being of the nature that they were still found ways of giving the children chocolate and sweets from their rations. If a home was required as a headquarters, or multiple homes as billets for the battalion, the family were given 30 minutes to vacate the building and move to a neighbour. In some cases they were confined to one room or floor of the home if it were thought that they could be trusted. Although plundering homes was forbidden, taking useful items such as cameras, watches etc. seems to have been accepted.

Note

1   See Addendum III – Listing Citations and Reports

23

News from the BBC

Most evenings the family still sat around the old wooden encased valve radio listening to the six o'clock BBC news. The news of the war was encouraging enough to lift the spirits, it was surely nearly over, and Basil would soon be home safely. There were constant reports of huge bomber attacks on German cities, including Bremen, Hamburg, Keil and even Berlin itself. The Russians had reached the river Danube and were within five miles of Vienna. They had cleared all of Hungary of German troops. Our own troops were advancing deep into Germany and north into Holland. In the pacific theatre, the Americans had been slowly leapfrogging islands towards Japan and had a foothold on the island of Okinawa. The offshore fleet at Okinawa, that included some British aircraft carriers and supporting ships, were suffering attack after attack by Japanese kamikaze aircraft. In Burma the Japanese army had been cut off by Indian troops and in Italy things were finally going well.

Lillian had also heard the BBC radio news reporting that all resistance in Germany had virtually ceased. This must have come as a huge relief to Lillian back home in Cumnor. Finally, she could relax a little. Her youngest boy was still safe, she had been receiving sporadic little brown postcards that said nothing more than he was safe and had received her last letter. It was enough to allay any thoughts that he may have come to harm but did little to stop her worry. The news that the war appeared to be nearly over must have raised her hopes. Neither Lillian, or anyone in the family, nor the war weary nation could have been prepared for the BBC radio news story that was about to break.

On the 12th of April the advancing troops of the 11th Armoured Division, attacking north towards Hamburg, way to the east of Basil and the Guards Armoured Division, were confronted with two German officers waving a white flag. They warned the troops that there was a large camp full of seriously ill people who should not be allowed to roam the countryside because of danger of disease. The Germans were prepared to withdraw from the area of the camp so that no fighting need take place around it. These negotiations stalled when the Germans would not agree to withdrawing far enough to prevent the camp ending up in the middle of an artillery duel. Eventually a truce was negotiated which included an agreement that no fighting would take place within a 48 Km exclusion zone around the camp. Around noon on the 15th a British delegation entered the camp to assess the condition. Joseph Crammer, the camp commandant showed them around the camp. He appeared indifferent and unashamed. The horror of what they saw shocked them to the core. There were various piles of thousands of rotting, stinking corpses lying all over the camp and a huge pit half full of corpses together with signs of other filled in mass graves. The smell of the camp was overpowering. The pitiful living looked like walking skeletons in stripped pyjamas and were crammed into long wooden huts suitable for 80 prisoners but containing as many as 1,000. The camp was the infamous Belsen Concentration Camp.

No one has ever had the words to do justice to explaining the horrors of that place. Richard Dimbleby who was a BBC Reporter travelling with fighting troops, arrived a couple of days after the liberation and produced a radio broadcast that came close to illustrating the true horrors he saw there. He was not authorised to do the broadcast until he threatened to resign.

The radio broadcast went out on the BBC news on the 17th of April. The report beggared belief to Lillian and everyone hearing it. How could any human do that to another? It became the talk of the nation.[1]

Note

1 The harrowing broadcast can be heard by searching online in the BBC archives.

24

A long hard slog

According to the war diary, on the 17th of April 1945 the Guards Armoured Division (including Basil and the battalion) changed to the command of XII Corps. Their northerly advance on Bremen was cancelled and redirected eastward. The official plan being that they would instead sever the autobahn between Bremen and Hamburg. This dramatic change of plan may well have in part been influenced by the humanitarian emergency arising at Belsen. Their rest at Emstek was cut short and plans made to head east. The long drive through already captured ground took them to a concentration area at Eilstorf less than 30 miles from Belsen concentration camp.

The war diary makes no mention of Belsen nor of 4 Company in the four days from their arrival at Emstek until the afternoon of the 19th of April. (It does go on to detail a successful attack by 3 Company on Neuenkirchen and 2 Company on Visselhövede).[1]

Basil and 4 Company's next mention was when they

attacked Tewel with 2 Squadron tanks on the 19th. At Tewel they met quite stiff resistance requiring an artillery bombardment to facilitate their attack which reduced the houses to rubble. That night 4 Company were attacked by a strong patrol. They waited until the Germans had come within a few yards before opening fire and the patrol was no more. They netted 87 Prisoners of War all from the German 2nd Marine Division, who were mostly redeployed submariners.

The 20th of April showed rapid movement through the villages of Hemslingen, Deepen, and Westervesede, with only light opposition. The latter was surrendered by the Bürgermeister during the night. The next town, Scheeßel was held but following a cheeky telephone call to the Bürgermeister, the town surrendered. The Bürgermeister, in an act of incredible bravery, rode on the lead tank, oblivious to the light rain falling all day, wielding a white flag to prove his good faith. 4 Company took up position on the bridge to the north of the town. The other companies effectively sealing off the town against counterattack. It transpired that Scheeßel contained a large German hospital.

The next town Rotenberg, much larger than Scheeßel, was also a hospital town. An attempt to encourage the surrender of the town failed and the message sent back was that the town would be defended to the last man. The size of the town meant that the Coldstream Group (1st Battalion tanks and Basil's battalion) were teamed up with the Scots and Welsh Guards group for a joint attack. 3 Company-3 Squadron tanks fought their way through the woods to the start line for the attack. Unfortunately, Captain Liddell was killed there before even knowing that he was to receive the

Victoria Cross for his action in capturing the bridge a few weeks before. The strong defence of the town required that the attack be postponed until the next day.

The battalion were given the job of capturing the northern half of Rotenburg, attacking from east to west. Basil and 4 Company were to attack and capture the houses and streets to the right of the main road, 2 Company to the left. They were to be supported by 1 Squadron tanks and plenty of artillery support. The attack went in at 9.30am in the light rain of another dull morning. After a heavy barrage both companies quickly reached their objectives and by noon the whole town was consolidated, however a few sporadic skirmishes continued when defenders were found in cellars. Part of the reason the defenders conceded relatively easily was the use of a flame thrower by one of the supporting companies which had been brought up to help a tank that had been hit by a panzerfaust. The flame hit a German soldier and killed him instantly, and mercifully, from shock. This prompted multiple surrenders. By 4.00pm they were relieved, and they returned to Scheeßel for the night and a welcome rest the following day.

This would have been the first time Basil and the boys would have seen a flamethrower in action and it must have had an impact on them. It's hard to imagine the gruesome sight they must have seen, never to be unseen.

Only one guardsman was killed but twenty were wounded, mostly from shelling. Over 1,000 prisoners of war were taken. The Commandant of Rotenburg, who had failed to carry out his order to defend to the last man later committed suicide by deliberately falling out of a railway truck and breaking his neck. German losses were very severe.

The 24th of April heralded a beautiful sunny day. The battalion were temporarily passed to the command of the 5th Brigade to pair with the Grenadiers to attack the town of Zeven. They had considerable resources available to them, including two squadrons of Mitchell bombers that in the event were not called upon, artillery, mortars, and flamethrowers – again. The Grenadiers were given the job of capturing the northern half of the town and the battalion, the southern half. They assembled in the small village of Wiersdorf amongst its ruined houses. After a heavy artillery bombardment, at 11am they advanced to the start line at the edge of the village. Basil and 4 Company were to lead the attack on the left of the road into Zeven, and 1 Company on the right, both with tanks in support. The rest of the battalion were to follow on behind.

At 11.50am they advanced. Basil and 4 Company immediately ran into the enemy in the wood in front of the town. They cleared the wood without difficulty but then ran into a 'Jagdpanther' self-propelled gun, which they knocked out and captured the crew. These were fearsome machines and very difficult for the allies to defeat due to their sheer size and dense armour, as such they presented a terrifying sight. To disable such a machine required stalking of it until at near point-blank range before firing a PIAT (projector, infantry, anti-tank – the British version of the Bazooka) at its weakest point. Yet another first and spine chilling experience for Basil and the boys!

Within an hour both companies were at their respective objectives, 4 Company in the Cemetery off *Kirchhofsallee*. The Grenadiers were held up due to a blown bridge. After a short while the Germans launched a counterattack, which was broken up by artillery fire, but by mid-afternoon the southern half of the town was under the battalion's control. The Grenadiers finally secured the northern half by midnight. Throughout the attack and into the evening the Germans shelled the town with nebelwerfers and 88s, causing casualties.

The defenders were from the Großdeutschland Regiment who had very limited tank support and had only arrived at the town the day before. 102 of them became prisoners of war. It is not known how many were killed or wounded.

Now returned to the 32nd Brigade, on the 26th of April, in the bright spring sunshine, the battalion moved four miles westwards towards Bremen into positions in the village of Badenstedt in preparation for an attack on the village of Wental the next day. The attack met no opposition so Basil and 4 Company with 3 Squadron tanks took up positions in the village and endured a now wet miserable overcast day. They remained there until travelling back with the battalion through Zeven and northeast to an area near Hollenbeck on the following day. This last move was in readiness to advance north on the town of Stade, as Bremen had finally been captured. The advance moved rapidly, meeting very weak opposition. 4 Company, now paired with 2 Squadron tanks, moved into the village of Deinste on Monday the 30th of April where they remained for a few days for an impromptu, unexpected rest due to the road to Stade being mined and bridges blown taking considerable time to repair. The rain had now turned to hail, and the air temperature had dropped making the first two days stay more of a challenge than a pleasure.

Not far from them, the Grenadiers had liberated

Sandbostel Concentration Camp containing 22,000 emaciated and diseased inmates.

That night news came through that Hitler and Goebbels were dead! The war seemed at last to be petering out.

The armed forces mail service must have caught up with them as Basil had received a letter that would have arrived on or around Wednesday the 2nd of May. It would have been a birthday card from Lillian and possibly a small gift as it was his 19th Birthday! It must have seemed surreal to him, on a fine sunny day at last, opening his birthday card with his mates around him in a village untouched by the fighting so far away from home. After weeks of nonstop movement, of almost daily terrifying and nerve shattering contact with the enemy, and with the news that Hitler was dead and the war almost over, his emotions must have been in overdrive. It would have been the first tangible contact with home for weeks and sent with love on his birthday. His reply to Lillian could only come in the form of a brown 'field service card'. It would only allow him to cross out lines that weren't applicable leaving the message to read *"I am quite well and am going on well. I have received your letter dated 28.4.45. Letter follows at first opportunity."* In the collection of letters I have, this is the only example of these bland 'field service cards', although I suspect Basil had sent several during his time on active service. This form of communication home was all that was allowed for security reasons.

Stade had surrendered on the 1st of May, and German forces were mostly across the river Oste forming a new defence line. A few were still south of the river around the small town of Himmelpforten. The translation being 'The gates of heaven'. As a result, the battalion's objective was to

NOTHING is to be written on this side except the date and signature of the sender. Sentences not required may be erased. If anything else is added the post card will be destroyed.

[Postage must be prepaid on any letter or post card addressed to the sender of this card.]

I am quite well.

I have been admitted into hospital

{ sick } and am going on well.

{ wounded } and hope to be discharged soon.

I am being sent down to the base.

I have received your { letter dated 28 · 4 · 45

telegram „

parcel „

Letter follows at first opportunity.

I have received no letter from you

{ lately

{ for a long time.

Signature only }

Date B. Bateman

Forms/A2042/7.
Wt. 18709/314 45,000M. 7/41. W. & S. Ld. 81-728. 102320P.

attack and capture the town. However, it was soon established that the Germans had pulled back across the bridge over the Oste river a few miles beyond. The attack was cancelled, and only 4 Company together with 3 Squadron tanks were ordered forward to occupy the 'The gates of heaven'.

The Oste bridge was reported still intact and passable so at 11.30am on Friday the 4th of May 1945, Basil and 4 Company advanced, riding on 3 Squadron tanks, to occupy it and the village of Hechthausen across the river. This was an important bridge to the advance as it opened up a route into northwest Germany as far as Cuxhaven and the North Sea. Any intact bridge was a prize worth chasing as the time spent building a temporary bridge gave the enemy time to arrange a strong defence the other side.

As they approached the bridge in the early afternoon, still riding on the tanks there was a terrific explosion. The massive blast disintegrated one of the tanks ahead of them and atomised the tank crew. Two of 4 Company's guardsmen were also wounded and many of the others blown to the ground. It turned out to be a sea mine and the resulting crater was over sixty feet wide.

There had been other examples of the use of sea mines in the area. The redeployed sailors they were now fighting against had brought their expertise in sea mines with them. Basil and the boys must have been shaken to the core, stunned, and deafened by this unexpected and monstrous blast, much larger than any other they had previously experienced. They still had to edge around the huge crater and walk over the bridge to occupy the village.

That evening the war diary states:

2300 Hours Message received from Brigade:- "Germans surrendered unconditionally at 1820 hours 4 May. Hostilities on all sectors Army front will cease at 0800 hours today. No, repeat NO, advance beyond present front line without orders from this H.Q."

Basil, George, Mansel, Fred and Paul had fought one of the last actions of the war in Europe! They had advanced further north into Germany than most other allied troops. Since crossing the Rhine, the battalion had travelled over 400 miles and fought multiple battles.

Since their all too brief rest at Emstek they had lost another 20 dead, (4 from 4 Company) and 67 wounded (7 from 4 Company). This all too depressing attrition has been likened to the game of musical chairs, the elimination process being a complete lottery as who would live, die, or be maimed.

The last edition of the Brussels Sprout newsletter, on the 1st of May 1945 gave a resume of these events.[2]

Note

1   It is this crucial gap in the war diary that fails to have any mention of Basil's 4 Company is discussed further in Addendum 1, as the family story has always been very specific about Basil having entered Belsen and spent time guarding SS Guards whilst they buried the emaciated dead there.
2   Citations and Reports are listed in Addendum III

25

VE Day in Germany

The next day Basil and 4 Company left Hechthausen and returned to Deinste for a couple more day's rest.

A plan was being formed whereby the Coldstream Guards were to make their way north to the airfield at Cuxhaven where they would receive the surrender of the German 7th Parachute Division. These were the very soldiers they had been fighting at many of the fierce engagements since Metzekath and across Germany, that had so bravely held onto their home ground to the last man on so many occasions, and were yet still, a well-equipped and potent force of elite troops. The finest troops in the German Army at that time. They had refused to surrender to any troops other than the Coldstream Guards, such was the respect they held for their British foe. The Scots and Welsh groups were to make their way to the port of Cuxhaven to take the surrender of the naval and other forces there.

On the morning of Monday, the 7th of May Basil and the boys rumbled forward towards Cuxhaven airfield kicking up clouds of dust rising high in the morning sunshine, creating a surreal vision of the long column of TCLs, armoured cars, universal carriers, tanks, self propelled guns, and all other paraphernalia of the Coldstream Group. They passed through village after village full of these troops, still 'dug in' in their defensive positions silently staring blankly at them as they passed. They passed long columns of horse drawn transport heading towards the airfield, and officers in staff cars. They even anxiously drove past an armoured flak train with the Germans still manning it, glaring at them. A battery from the anti-tank regiment were sent to deal with this potentially dangerous situation. It transpired that they were reluctant to lay down their arms as they were very close to a Russian forced labour camp and feared reprisal attack from them. It must have been yet another incongruous experience and totally unnerving to think that although both sides were ordered to not fire, any unfortunate accidental firing of a weapon from either side could have resulted in carnage. The atmosphere along the whole journey must have been highly charged, only two days before they were sworn enemies. One cannot 'switch off' that easily.

The boys arrived at Cuxhaven airfield late that day and set up positions ready to receive the surrender the next morning, 4 Company being located at the road and rail crossing to the north of the airfield.

Under troubled skies, the morning saw the start of the arrival of the 7th Parachute Division. They entered the airfield strewn with broken aircraft, marching proudly in columns and looking like a far from beaten foe. Their heavy guns, tracked vehicles, lorries, horse drawn wagons and miscellaneous equipment rolled in and neatly lined up. It took several hours but by late afternoon the paratroopers were all formed up in front of the empty hangers, in orderly lines with officers in front. Behind them row upon row of their equipment, far more than was expected or known about cast a dark shadow over the whole airfield. At 4.00pm, with full cooperation and good discipline they took the salute and were marched off to be searched and billeted nearby. Only a few needed reminding that the surrender was unconditional. The Officers were separated off. It was an impressive and formal ceremony.

So that was Basil and the boys' VE Day experience. No great celebrations; it would probably take a long time to fully sink in.

26

Life in peacetime Germany

The battalion remained at Cuxhaven airfield for a further ten days to administer the screening of the German troops, reorganise various ammunition and food dumps, and to round up any German army stragglers. They then moved back to the area around Westervesede on the 19th of May. Basil and 4 Company were based at Vahlde, the other Companies being nearby. There they had an extended stay to collect up equipment and ammunition still lying about the countryside, and general 'policing' of the area. They also got the rest they had deserved for so long.

Towards the end of the war Himmler, the feared head of the nazi SS, and trusted co-conspirator of Adolf Hitler, took over the management of the defence of north-west Germany. The general theme of his defence plan was that of – no retreat, fight to the last man and bullet, and no surrender of any town or village. Any failure to meet this order was to face dishonour and death. All senior German army officers and civilian burgomasters were under no illusion that failure to carry out these orders would not only mean their own death and dishonour, but also that of their family still in areas under nazi control. The feared Gestapo, (nazi secret police) and the SS were still very organised and active till the end of the war and were very adept at arrest and public hanging of those failing to 'do their duty'. In addition, the 'Hitler Youth' were spurred on under Himmler's control to act in a similar way. For example, the town of Bützfleth begged Basil's Guards Armoured Division to take over the town as the civilians were being murdered by the local Hitler Youth.

As a consequence of this terrible situation, the occupation troops were in many areas of north-west Germany regarded as 'tolerated liberators'. Seen by the civilian public as the only chance of offering a safe and secure environment against the backdrop of food shortage and displaced forced labour camp inmates from all over Europe, filled with anger and intent on revenge. There were some of course that viewed them with hostility. Some of the men, after their initial fear of the conquering armies, regressed to their former arrogance whilst the majority of the women tended to quietly welcome their presence, accepting chocolate bars and sweets for their children. However, it was common for women who overly fraternised with the British troops to be ostracised. It was to this strained and complex social situation that Basil and the boys found themselves in when they entered Vahlde.

Little is recorded of their stay in this idyllic rural location, but in the letters collection there are a couple of small black and white photographs taken in rural locations that were possibly taken during the stay there. Apart from carrying out the job in hand, it must have been a good time for re-equipping and the predictable smartening up and fitness regime so exacting for the Coldstream Guards. The mail delivery must have caught up with them. The first full letter home in the letter collection is dated Wednesday 6th of June 1945, ironically a year to the day since D-Day:[1]

"My Dear Mum, Just a few lines to let you know I am O.K. and received your letter. We are getting plenty of entertainment lately last Thursday I went to an ENSA show and it was very good, Friday I went to the pictures and saw Janeie it was quite a good film, we have got a NAAFI here now so that we can have a tea and a wod for supper we can also have beer but its just like cricket's water. It going to be a big day for us on Saturday the 1st Batt Cold. Are handing in their tanks, Monty's coming to take the fare well salute to the tanks. Well mum not a lot to say hope everyone at home are O.K. hope Dans having a nice time. cherio for now. Lots of love xxxxx Basil xxxxxx"[1]

ENSA stands for 'Entertainments National Service Association' who provided entertainment for the troops throughout the war. 'Janie' (not 'Janeie') was a film produced in 1944. Janie is a free-spirited teenage girl living in a small town. The war brings the establishment of an army camp nearby, which is opposed by her father, the local newspaper publisher. Janie and her friends have their hearts set afire by the prospect of so many young soldiers so close. She enjoys dating an army man, which makes her younger local boyfriend jealous. Starring Joyce Reynolds as Janie Conway and Robert Hutton.

The 'farewell salute to the tanks' Basil mentions in the

letter was a huge parade, referred to as 'The farewell to armour parade', held on the airfield nearby at Rotenberg on Saturday the 9th of June. It was presided over by Field Marshal Montgomery (Monty) himself. The various Guards regiments of the British army were historically all infantry regiments. In 1941 the Guards Armoured Division was formed requiring some of the battalions to be converted to tanks. For example, the 1st Battalion Coldstream. This parade was to provide a rather theatrical way of taking the severely worn out tanks away and returning the battalions to infantry. The tanks were driven in tight formation across the airfield and over a ridge in the ground till out of sight of the spectators. A few minutes later their crews marched back over the ridge and were subjected to a speech by Monty, praising and thanking them for their service. Basil was present at this parade, standing to attention throughout.

Their time at this relatively rural backwater ended when the orders came to take over responsibility for the Cologne area from the Americans. When they arrived on the 17th of June, they found Cologne in a state of total ruin. Like all German cities that had been so heavily bombed, it stank from the destroyed sewers and thousands of decomposed bodies buried under the collapsed buildings. The streets were filled with rubble and the ruined remains of the famous cathedral stood as testimony to the devastation caused by the numerous 1,000 bomber raids it endured. Around the city the entire infrastructure of bridges, roads, telephone lines, power lines and power stations were destroyed. The situation was far worse than in the rural areas with their undamaged buildings where food could be grown in gardens. The survivors of the air raids and the street fighting were living in cellars, windowless rooms, or even rooms with walls missing. Food was in short supply and the city a very unsafe place to be. Armed gangs of foreign displaced persons, mainly Russian and Polish, roamed the streets with hatred of anyone German. The black market created its own problems with armed gangs regularly raiding food dumps. Crime and violence, including car theft, rape, and murder was rife. There was also the expected threat of 'werewolf' activity and sabotage, but none had manifested itself.[2]

The battalion took over the area of Weiden, towards the outskirts of the town to use as their living quarters as there were no usable undamaged buildings in Cologne itself. The war diary states the duties they were expected to perform:

'The guard duties occupy two Companies and half of Support Company, thus allowing a change over of alternate three days on, four days off, four days on, three days off. The Vulnerable Premises are as follows:- OSSENDORF Camp (9,000 Russians); ETMAL Camp (4,600 Poles); The RHINE Bridge; The Prison; Telephone Exchanges; Food Warehouses......

Basil and the boys clearly had their work cut out but nothing like as bad as the situations they had found themselves in throughout the earlier part of the year. Being the Coldstream Guards, they did of course have to maintain their immaculate presentation which involved lots of pressing of uniform and 'bulling' of leather. Penty of recreation time made up for that. It is whilst he was in Cologne that he met his German girlfriend he refers to as 'the fraulien'. Perhaps he thought of her as his *Janie*.

The 5th Battalion had been formed to expand the number of Coldstream regiments for war time. Now that peace had come the days of the need for them was fast coming to an end. Tuesday the 10th of July saw a 'Farewell to 5th Battalion parade' at the sports stadium in Cologne. A reporter for the Guards Armoured Division's newsletter – 'The News Guardian' wrote:

"Fighting Fifths" Last Parade, General Allan ADAIR Pays Tribute.

Tonight we bade farewell to the 5th Battalion COLDSTREAM GUARDS, the "Fighting Fifth", as the Divisional Commander so aptly described them. Their fighting days over, men of the Battalion are being gradually absorbed into other Battalions. Tonight was the farewell parade, with the whole Battalion present, and Major-General Allan ADAIR, C.B., D.S.O., M.C., took the salute and later paid tribute to the fighting qualities of the Battalion. Unfortunately the Regimental Band was away in HAMBURG, but deputising for them was the Battalion Corps of Drums under Drum-Major OSBORNE which gave yeoman service and earned bouquets from everyone. Sharp at 6.30 p.m., the General arrived, and the Commanding Officer, Lieutenant-Colonel E.R. HILL D.S.O, gave the general salute. General ADAIR came down from the stand, acknowledged Colonel Roddy's salute, shook hands with him and then began his inspection.............. The inspection lasted 28 minutes and General ADAIR stopped to speak to many men in the ranks. On his return to the stand the General moved to the microphone preparatory to making his speech. His opening sentence was "Right-hand man of the rear rank, raise your hand." Away in the distance a hand appeared, and we knew that the Battalion signallers had done a good job. Afterwards General ADAIR moved down to the saluting base and the end was near. The Commanding Officer ordered "slope arms", and the Battalion could never have sloped arms better than on this particular occasion. Then – "move to the right, right turn" and a few seconds later the Battalion was on its last journey to the tune of the Regimental Slow March. Away they marched, all heads turned to the left towards the General and as they were about to disappear from view the Drums broke into "Auld Lang Syne". It was all very dramatic, and as the guardsmen reached the exit to the stadium, the music became fainter and fainter until the last man was out of sight. The Drums counter-marched, halted and the strains of "Auld Lang Syne" died away. A few seconds later the Drums returned, playing the Regimental March. They marched across the stadium and wheeled to a halt in front of the saluting base. Drum-Major OSBORNE asked for permission to dismiss and the Ceremony was complete. Another glorious page in the annals of the COLDSTREAM GUARDS had been written.

This is what Adair, Commander in Chief of the 5th Battalion, said in his speech:

"Now that the war is over we come to a period of change and re-organisation. The old firm has to be

broken up. We have said farewell to our tanks and now to-night we have to say farewell to the fighting 5th Battalion. It is in many ways a sad moment but don't forget the war is won and such re-organisations are inevitable. Now I feel no one is more qualified than I, who had the great fortune to command the Division throughout this Campaign to say to you 'Well done'. I have seen you fight in every battle throughout the Campaign. For a moment let us turn back to those many battles you fought, and I would say here and now that the 5th Battalion COLDSTREAM have fought in more battles than any other Battalion in the DIVISION, and the Battalion has gone from strength to strength... Now I pass on to Operation VERITABLE. That battle of yours in smashing the WESEL bridgehead has become world famous. That relentless advance on a very narrow front – it had to be narrow – against strong opposition, backed up by the tanks as usual, somehow has struck the imagination and indeed it was a very fine action. Then on the 30th March we crossed the RHINE and the end of the Campaign was in sight. But as you know well, plenty of tough fighting remained for us............... You passed on and captured ROTENBURG, you went on to capture ZEVEN, and finally you crossed the OSTE CANAL, and V.E. DAY came along. What could be a more fitting climax than the disarming of your old opponents the 7th Para Division by yourselves and the 1st Battalion. It was a fitting climax to a great Campaign. Now in a few minutes you will be marching off to the strains of 'Auld

Lang Syne'. Old teams will perhaps be broken up in a few days, old friendships for the moment severed, but remember each one of you, wherever you may be or wherever you go, you have been sent with a very high standard of conduct and achievement in this Battalion, and it is always up to you individually to keep that standard up. I congratulate Colonel Roddy who has led you so well, and I congratulate every one of you. You have added a proud chapter to the history of your Regiment. And I say you have proved that the 5th is well worth of your Motto: 'Nulli Secundus'."

From then on, although still in Cologne, the battalion's status was changed to that of a 'demobilisation battalion'. The war diary has no record of any 'policing activity' for the remainder of the month so they must have had been relieved from those duties and hence the opportunity to grant leave home for some arose.

The second letter from the collection, dated Saturday 21st of July 1945 began:

"Dear Mum, Just a few lines to let you know I am alright. Well mum they say we shall start on our way to England on Monday, I hope you got the letter in time on Thursday so that you wouldn't wait up for me. We are having some lovely weather lately hope you are having the same. Well mum not much news please excuse this short letter. cherio for now Lots of love Basil xxxxxxxxxxxxx"

Basil must have had a strong impression that he was to

go on Privilege Leave. For some reason that didn't happen and was postponed. It was most likely, and cruelly for Basil, due to the forthcoming huge parade to take place in Brussels to celebrate the battalion's liberation of the city back in 1944. On the 28th of July a battalion contingent 220 strong, which probably included Basil, left Weiden in motor transport and off to Brussels for the Guards Armoured Division parade through the city. This was a formal event and must have been an amazing experience for him, with the population turning out to cheer and wave, although he must have thought it no compensation for his delayed leave.

Life in Cologne ground on. The war diary shows that they returned to being very busy with their 'policing role', for example:

7 August
In conjunction with 2nd HOUSEHOLD CAVALRY REGIMENT a sweep was made through the STAATFOREST BENRATH 3373, to round up stray Displaced Persons and other lawless elements that have been responsible for local looting.

On the 15th of August, Basil was finally granted 'Privilege Leave' to return back home. He must have been ecstatic at the news.

Note

1 All letters have been reproduced with the spelling and grammar as per the original hand-written letters.
2 Information had been received that the Nazi leadership had planned

that in the event of Germany losing the war that 'Werewolf' groups would be expected to be formed from fanatical groups of loyal Nazis.

27

An overdue home leave

In Basil's 'pay book' amid the collection of letters, it is recorded that he was granted 'privilege leave' for the 15th of August 1945. There is no entry to indicate the length or end of this leave. Perhaps due to the disorganisation associated with the imminent disbanding of the regiment. It was likely that leave was for seven days, as was the norm. It is not recorded how he travelled home but he clearly knocked hard on the door, startling Hazel as is clear from his letters. Floss would have raced to the door to greet him followed by everyone else in the house. Lillian's last sight of him was from back in November so this must have been the most joyous of home comings. Her youngest boy was home; he had survived the war. He would have been very content to be living the long yearned for experience that at many of his most perilous times, he would have been convinced would never happen.

She had been saving up for months to buy him a gold signet ring so that he could have one just like his mates. She had hoped to give it to him on his birthday but as he had no expectation of 'privilege leave' around his birthday she decided to wait until he did come home as to risk posting such a valuable item was unthinkable. Now was the time to present it to him. He was thrilled and it fitted his large ring finger perfectly.

Lillian would have seen a change in her boy; he had seen and done too much to ever be quite the same innocent he once was. Like all soldiers returning from war, he would have felt somehow different, remote, and unable to relate to the trivia of the simple life that was once his. His head would still have been with his mates, with the sights and sounds and smells of a far off place. She would have fussed over him the entire time he was home and fed him the best food she could afford. Nothing too good for her long absent boy. A very proud and relieved mother. He was home and the war was long over. He would have told her all about Cologne, the state of the devastation, of the interactions he had with the locals, of the exploits of his mates, of his girlfriend, of his experiences while guarding the prison and the bridge. He most likely would not have felt able to tell her about the violence, terror, and deprivation he suffered throughout the worst of the Rhineland battles or the drawn-out fighting advance across north-west Germany, or even the unstable situation in Cologne. None of them did, particularly those who had seen the worst of the fighting and the depraved depths of humanity. I'm sure Lillian would have gained enough information in any case to worry about his safety when he got back.

However, there was a lot of talk about the upcoming Nurenburg trials at this time and in particular the culpability for the concentration camps. As it was highly topical, it is at this point that Basil may well have recounted his experiences to the family in respect of Sandbostel and Belsen.

This leave wouldn't have been complete without a trip to the farm to see his old workmates. "What's it like over there?" would surely have been the number one question they would have asked. Again, the unspeakable deprivation, horrors and deeds of fighting to the death, to kill or be killed on an almost daily basis for almost four months would not have passed his lips. Only those who were there could possibly comprehend that. He would have been far more likely to talk about the farms he encountered in Belgium, Holland and Germany. He would have told them of his pleasant stay in Opheylissem, of the friendly locals who cared so much for him, of the houses with barns attached where the animals were unseparated from the house, of the underlying smell of cattle whilst eating at the dinner table. He would have told them of the prosperous Dutch and German farms, of the smaller peasant farms, of the single cylinder small tractors with their deep booming thump-thump-thump as they crawled along heavily overladen with family and produce.

He may not have been able to mention the squalor of the farm at Buchholt or of the countless destroyed, desolate and smoke blackened farms, with ownerless barking dogs he would have passed through, where the livestock had roasted to death chained up in their stalls. Of the lucky surviving cows mewing painfully with no one to milk them, roaming amongst the bloated stinking bodies of the dead with their legs sticking out almost comically. These were the images, sounds and smells he, his mates and all those involved in the fighting in the last months of the war would have to live silently with for life.

The leave may have been short but like most soldiers he would have been glad to get back to his mates and his new perception of life.

Mansel Godwin in Germany

Mansel and Basil

4 Company 1st Battalion Coldstream in Germany Nov – Dec 1945
(Basil third row on right)

28

Back in Germany

Basil returned from leave to a busy battalion, just in time for the next operation. The war diary states:

24 August
Operation TARANTULA – a 24 hours road check to examine the passes of all civilian vehicles and impound the illegal ones. Several arrests were made.
The chief events during the month have been:-
All small arms ammunition has now been collected and moved from the Battalion area.
The OSSENDORF Camp has been cleared of its 4,600 Russian Displaced Persons who have been repatriated.
A 24 hour night Patrol has been set up in COLOGNE to prevent the looting of food warehouses, several of which have been attacked recently.
Routine Curfew checks and checks on civilian and Displaced Persons continue. Looting and Crimes with violence have decreased but are still very frequent.

Company route marches to the area of Lake CONSTANCE have been organised and two of the Companies have now made their marches.

The company route marches mentioned in the war diary would have made a welcome adventure for Basil and the boys. In the envelope of documents and photographs I found a postcard relating to Ligny en Barrois in France. On the rear was written *'passed through here'*. Ligny en Barrois is a picturesque village to the west of Lake Constance. It is likely that the battalion route marches involved a round trip that took in Ligny en Barrois.

This is the last letter in the collection he sent whilst part of the 5th Battalion, sent on Friday the 5th of October:

"Dearest Mother, Many thanks for your very welcome letter I received to-day. "Friday". I am sorry I have been so late at writing again but I have been on another guard. You are right when you say we are doing a

lot of guards but it will only last another month. This batt breaks up in another month and another regiment relieves us. Wherever we go we won't have to do so many guards as we are doing now. Still the guards are not too bad its only a case of being there in case anything does happen. Well I can just imagine Marjorie Ratcliffe's father doing what he did at her wedding. I wonder what he managed so comical at his own wedding. Tell Mary to lay off the booze and leave a spot for me………… It seems as though I won't have a chance for harvest leave for most of the fellows in the Batt that did have it are back now. I heard about the train crash, do they suspect foul play at all. Thank Mary for me for the pin up girl I have quite a large collection now, no need for wallpaper. Well mother I think I will sign off now as I have boots "etc" to polish and what a polish. So cherio for now and God Bless You. Your Everloving Son Basil xxxxxxxxxxx xxxxxxxxxx

We may never know what Marjorie Ratcliffe's father did, and it sounded like Mary was still celebrating VE Day. The rail crash he makes reference to was the Bourne End rail crash which occurred on the 30th of September, when an overnight sleeper train from Perth to London derailed due to driver error. Forty-three people were killed, making it Britain's joint seventh worst rail disaster in terms of death toll.

During these last few weeks of the battalion's life, up until the 31st of October, Basil was to see his closest friends slowly being given notice of postings to other units. George was to transfer to the Provost Company of the Guards Division based in Brussels, Paul to transfer to the 3rd Battalion

Coldstream Guards, Mansel to transfer to the Coldstream Guards Divisional College based in Bonn. Only Fred was to remain with Basil, and they were in turn to be transferred to 4 Company of the 1st Battalion Coldstream Guards.

This must have been the most depressing time of his entire time in uniform. They had looked after each other through unimaginable terror, hardships, and depravations of every kind. They were truly, as Mansel's son was later to coin, *a band of brothers*. Nothing could ever again eclipse this experience in their lives in every sense. They had all been conscripted to fight the Germans, to fight for freedom, for their king and country. Like all young men placed in such circumstances, they actually fought for the sake of each other, to support and protect each other, to never let their mates down. They fought for 'the duration of the war', they didn't sign up to the peacetime existence of a guard's regiment. The 5th Battalion that he loved and felt a part of had gone.

Two weeks into life in the new battalion, Basil sent a series of letters home. They give a great insight into his experiences, thoughts and feelings, love life, and the situation in general at that time, and in particular his displeasure at being in the 1st Battalion in peacetime:

Wednesday 14th November 1945
Dear Mum, many thanks for your two most welcome letters which I have received. I received one yesterday and one about three days ago. I am very sorry I have not answered them before now. I have been that busy lately getting my kit up to the standard of this battalion. I am fed up of this place already we are doing route marches, cross country runs, drill parades, weapon

training and there is always plenty of kit to be shined. You would think we are training for war, not that the war is finished. It seems as though the weather here is the same as it is at home foggy, wet and very cold. Very pleased to hear about Hazels forthcoming baby, If it is a boy I will train him to be a guardsman (I don't think). I am very sorry I could not get a birthday card for you. I am hoping to get a present for you before I come on leave. If I can't, I will get you one while I am on leave. We had a lecture by the C.O. the other day he said we may be home early next year. I should get my leave next month. I hope to be home for xmas. (so get those cockerels ready). I am very pleased to hear you liked my photographs. I thought they were not good. I might look happy on the photograph, but I am not so happy now, there were six photographs but the fraulien took two of them. I did not see her when I left the fifth Battalion as she was away in the Russian zone. I expect she will have a shock when she gets back and finds that I have left there. We have a canteen here we can get plenty of tea without sugar, and cakes. They do not sell suppers there. If they did I would be there every night having a good tuck in. But still I have a good tuck in of cakes and tea, sometimes I have a pint when the tea is extra steady which nearly every night the beer is very steady but I have to quench my thirst with something. I will be glad when I get home for a good cup of tea and a drop of good English beer. I am enclosing a photograph of the inside of Cologne cathedral. As you can see it is knocked about a little bit. It is just like the yank to get in front of the camera. We have only moved

*about thirty miles further away from England. It only
takes four or five days for a letter to get from England
to this place. I doubt if those two men curly was talking
to came from this battalion, they have very likely got
stuck of jobs driving somewhere else. I wish I could
get another job somewhere away from the battalion. I
think **** is very lucky going to India I wish I was going
with him. Anything to get away from this Battalion. I
wish I could give up smoking as my ration of 110 cigs
a week only lasts me about five days. I received those
photographs of Grace and Danny I thought they were
very good. I have not received the cigs yet, I hope to get
them when I am short I am not short at the moment as
I have only just received my ration. Well mother this is
all the news for now as I will bring my short letter to a
close for now. Your loving son Basil xxxxxx xxxx*

Hazel had continued to live at home with Lillian even after
her marriage to Jim. He must have managed to get leave from
Foxhall Barracks at some point after the end of hostilities as
he and Hazel were able to announce her pregnancy just prior
to this letter. Sadly, the baby girl was still born.

Basil mentions 'the fraulien' but frustratingly never
provides her name. He must have met her while stationed in
Weiden, Cologne and it seems a sad quirk of fate that he never
got to see her again. She must have been very brave to have
dated a British soldier like Basil as many German women
who fraternised with British soldiers were ostracised. Both
Iris and Vera knew of her and believed her to have been very
special to him. I can only wonder if she ever found out what
had happened to Basil. I also wonder what Violet Smith back

Basil's photograph of Cologne Cathedral mentioned in his letter

home would have thought about it, and of course, whether she knew.

It is interesting to hear that Basil smoked cigarettes. It was understood that he never smoked at all, at least before he 'joined up'. Either he was using them as currency with his mates, or that it was just inevitable that he smoked given the traumas of war and perhaps just the need to fit in with many of those around him who smoked.

Saturday 24th November 1945
Dear Mother, Just a few lines in answer to your most

welcome letter which I have just received. This is the first letter I have received from you this week, I wrote to you in the week. There was no mail for this battalion for three days during the week, I guess it was held up for some reason or other. I'm afraid I won't be coming home as I told you previously, as we had a lecture the other day by one of our officers he said we will not be going back to England instead we are moving to Bergen or Denmark in the spring. Anyway, I am still hoping to get my leave around xmas time. I will be able to let you know in about 10 days time the date I will be coming on leave. I think it is a good idea for you to make the puddings a little early in case I do get home before xmas. Pleased to hear Ken got you a good cockerel for xmas. We have not had any fowl to eat since the war finished so it will be nice to get tucked into the cockerel........ I am sorry to hear you have not been too well lately I hope you are better by the time you get this letter. Jimmy was very lucky getting away with the charge of sleeping by the Absentees bed. If we got caught doing that we would get about fourteen days. They have not started to rebuild anything in Cologne yet, it will take about ten years to move the rubble before they can start building. We have got a very good place to live in, we are in a school it has not been touched by bombs. It is situated on top of a big hill. Mary should be ashamed of herself going with a Polish soldier, she wants to get away from him before I come on leave otherwise she will be getting her earhole clipped, as soon as I see her, (make sure you tell her what I have said) He might be polite but I have seen some of the things they have been doing to the girls out here. Also they cause more trouble than the Germans. Tell her to keep away from the foreigners. I am very pleased to hear Iris won't have anything to do with them. Well mom this is all the news for now so I will bring my short letter to a close, cherio for now. Your loving son Basil. xxxxxxxxxx xxxx

Cologne at the time of his letters was extremely violent and unsafe. The city had been bombed multiple times resulting in most of the buildings being reduced to rubble.[1] There were large numbers of armed 'displaced persons' roaming the streets, many intent on revenge against the German population. There were large camps in the area that had contained thousands of these 'displaced persons' who were mostly Polish and Russian. There were multiple reports of rape, murder, burglary and robbery. A large proportion of these crimes allegedly being committed by the 'displaced persons'. Basil's displeasure at Mary dating a Polish soldier was clearly based on his experiences in Cologne.

Tuesday 9th of December 1945
Dear Mother, many thanks for your most welcome letter which I have just received. I am more than pleased to hear you have recovered from your illness. I am enjoying the best of health but still browned off. We have just had an inspection by our C.O. we had to clean up every bit of our kit last night also repair any holes we had in our clothes. I came off guard yesterday morning, I was cleaning from when I came off till 10-30 at night. You can just imagine how browned off we

are. I believe it was because of the fog that I had no mail for three days, nobody else had any either. It is very rare that I go out at nights, I only go out once or twice a week to the cinema when I do go out I always have a couple of mates with me so there is no need to worry about me. As you can see I started this letter on Tuesday it is now Saturday. I had an inoculation just after I started this letter my arm got too stiff to write so I had to leave off till now. I should be able to make this a nice long letter as I have had another letter from you today. George is not with me now, he is in Brussels on the Military Police. I prefer to go to Denmark than do guards in London. The chaps who have done guards on the palace say it is terrible. It is only six more days to my leave, I am coming on the fourteenth not the nineteenth. I should be home on Sunday night. Tell Hazel I won't knock the door so hard next time. I am more than pleased to hear the pole is going back to Poland. I hope he stays there. Tell Hazel I have still got the ring I would not part with it for anything……. Cherio for now. Your loving son. Basil. Xxxxxxxxxxxxxx

Saturday the 12th of December 1945. Dear Mother, many thanks for your most welcome letter which I have just received. Also, I wish to thank you for the parcel which I received two days ago. My friend and I had a good tuck in of chocolate and apples. I guessed you would be surprised to hear from me again so soon. This company did not do any good in the drill competition. Support Coy came first they will be *entered for the divisions drill competition I hope they win. We had a big parade this morning to welcome the colours back to the battalion, after the parade we marched past the division's commander. The only thing I did not like was that I was very cold my fingers were numb after we had stood to attention for about fifteen minutes. It does not matter about the photographs for now, we will try to get some taken when I am on leave. By the way my leave has been put forward a few days, I will be coming on the 14th of December so I will be home on the 16th. That is if the ships are not cancelled owing to bad weather. I suppose you will be a little short yourself now that Hazel is only giving you £1 a week. I think it is a very good idea for Iris to buy some slacks now that the cold weather is coming. So Mary has not got rid of that Polish soldier, tell her the quicker she leaves him the better. Does Curly know that she is going with him, I am going to write and tell him about her, so she had better watch out for herself. If you are sending me another parcel any kind of cigs will do as I have got used to any kind by now. I have not heard from Curly, thanks for sending me his letter to read. I will write to him as soon as I get a few minutes to spare. I don't feel like writing much more this week as I have wrote three or four letters every day....... Well mother this is all the news for now so I will close cherio for now, Your loving son Basil xxxxxxx xxxxxxxxxx*

Basil did as he said and arrived home, knocking gently on the door this time. Iris attests that he was very ill, so ill that she couldn't believe he had made it home, that he spent all his time quietly in front of the fire being unable to get warm. The agonising deprivation of sleep, exposure to icy rain, sleet and snow that chilled him to the bone for days and nights on end, together with the abject terror of battle that he endured in fighting for his country, must have taken a considerable toll on his health, weight and possibly his immunity to infection. What is known is that Lillian took him to see Dr Dempsey, the family doctor very shortly after his arrival home. From that consultation he was immediately admitted to the Radcliffe Infirmary, Oxford. Either because he was still a serving soldier, or because the Radcliffe Infirmary recognised that he needed specialist treatment, he was transferred to Shaftesbury Military Hospital where he was initially diagnosed with Pyelitis, however this was later re-diagnosed as Tubercular Kidney (Renal Tuberculosis). His condition quickly deteriorated and finally lost his young life on the 22nd of January 1945, aged 19.

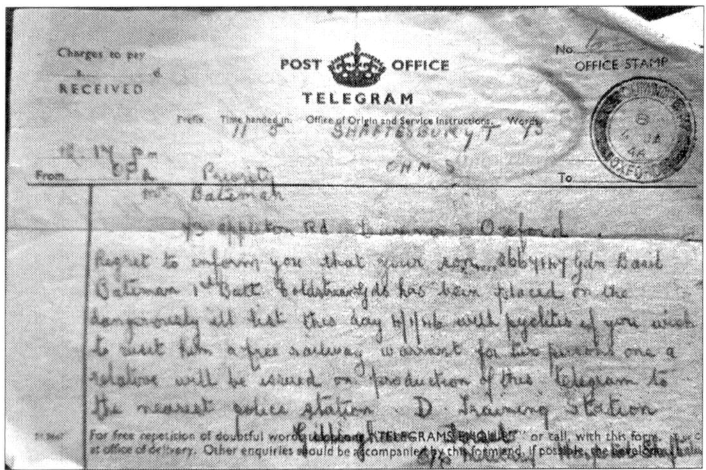

The Telegram informing that Basil was placed on the 'dangerously ill list' with Pylitis

No. 29/3/1/46.
(If replying, please quote above No.)

Army Form B. 104—82B.

Coldstream Guards Record Office,

73 Ashley Gardens, S.W.1.

23rd January, 19 46.

Madam,

It is my painful duty to inform you that a report has been received from the War Office notifying the death of :—

(No.) 2667147 (Rank) Guardsman

(Name) Basil Richard RACHMAN

(Regiment) Coldstream Guards

which occurred in the Military Hospital, Shaftesbury,

on the 22nd January, 1946

The report is to the effect that he Died from Tubercular Kidney

I am to express the sympathy and regret of the Army Council at the soldier's death in his Country's service.

I am,

Madam,

Mrs. Bateman,
73 Appleton Road,
Cumnor, Oxford,
Oxon.

Your obedient Servant,

John Charndable

Major,
Officer in Charge of Records.
Coldstream Guards T.A.

Military Death Certificate

Note

1   The Imperial War Museum have numerous photographs of Cologne in ruins, one example being Ref no. – FRE11580 which shows the badly damaged Cathedral surrounded by bombed out buildings, and the ruined bridge beyond

29

You don't find many about like him

After Basil's death, George Davidson had a short trip to Brussels on the 8th of February and by complete chance ran into Mansel Godwin. He wrote to Lillian the next day. A few days later she received the letter. It read:

My Dear Mrs Bateman, I was at a dance last night and I saw Mansel Godwin. He told me about Basil. I knew he had been very ill for some time. It was a great shock to me, as I've lost one of the best pals I ever had. You have my deepest sympathy. I got a newspaper cutting with a 'photo' which I got off Mansel. It is not very plain though, and I would be very pleased if you could let me have another one much plainer. Well Mrs Bateman I'm afraid there isn't a great more to say just now. If I can manage the time the next leave I get I shall come to see you. Understand it will be a rush visit. We only get 11 days so don't be disappointed if I can't make it. Well I'll close now. Once again I send my regrets. So Cherrio All my love George Davidson xxxx xxx.

Mansel had written within a few days of Basil's death to express his condolences, but the letter must have been lost. He wrote again:

Dear Mrs Bateman, had a letter from mother yesterday she said you did not say anything about my letter I wrote two or three weeks ago, maybe it has got lost in the post, hope you will get this all right. Very sorry to hear the news about Basil he was one of the best of pals you don't find many about like him. Mother say in her letter you were poorly hope you are getting better now, hope the rest of the family is in good health, hope to be able to get up to see you when I come next time. Should get my leave by the beginning of next month. We are moving up north soon don't quite know when. Will have got to write home also to Paul and the lads out there, wish we could all have got together again once more. Must stop now hope you will have got the other before you get this, still I know you would like to get a line from me Cheerio Mansel

Paul Hagan also wrote:

Dear Mrs Bateman, Many thanks for your lovely letter received tonight and I'm sorry to hear that the youngest daughter is ill. I sincerely hope that by the time this letter reaches you all that she is up and about again. It seems that everyones troubles come at once doesn't it. I am so pleased to hear that you have heard from George again as Basil and him were the very best of pals. I heard he was in the M.P.'s but didn't think he would like them but at the same time I think he always had a fancy for the Police. He should be better off than in this lot. I don't know if I told you in my last letter but I lost my third stripe a fortnight ago and am on a severe reprimand and otherwise 14 days C.B. What happened was that I was going to be made up on the Saturday, but on the Thursday night I was out on a road block and dozed off a couple of minutes whilst on Sentry. The Officer caught me and had me on a C.O's Orders, he told me I was lucky I didn't get a Court Marshal. The Company Commander then told me not to worry but to watch I didn't get into any more trouble as he would see that I get my third the next lot of Corporals that got made up. So I'm watching my Ps and Qs now. The weather here is glorious and absolutely scorching hot and today I spent my afternoon bathing in the hot springs at Baaden. It was lovely there and I thoroughly enjoyed myself the short time I was there. We have had the Colonel of the Regiment inspecting us this week and I'm sick of bulling and polishing brasses for him coming. Still we have to put up with these things I suppose. That just about covers all my news now so will close. I will love to have a photograph of Basil whenever you can send one. For the present Cherio And God Bless You All. Yours as always Paul

Some weeks later a formal white wooden cross marked 'Guardsman B. R. Bateman Coldstream Guards' was provided by the War Office. When that faded another was provided. When the Commonwealth War Graves Commission took over management of all war graves, a white marble headstone was provided which now stands very distinctively in the walled lower graveyard to the right of the Church. The inscription reads:

2667147 Guardsman B. R. Bateman Coldstream Guards 22nd January 1946 Age 19 'One of the Bravest One of the best God grant him now Eternal rest'

The stone war memorial, dedicated to the first world war dead, next to the school was updated by squeezing in '1939 – 1945' with difficulty under the much larger font '1914 – 1918'. 'B. R. Bateman' was added second from the top of the alphabetical list on the left flank of the memorial. Inside St Michael's Church the refurbished war memorial bears his name, again second from the top. At Botley school a small brass plaque, mounted on wood was placed above one of the internal double doors with Basil's name, together with the only other schoolboy to lose his life in the war, Sidney Willis, another Coldstreamer. Every year without fail Lillian attended the Remembrance Sunday Parade and placed a wooden cross with a poppy until too frail to do so. The family have taken over and every November a cross with a poppy is placed in the small, grassed area around the memorial. At Christmas time a wreath is placed on Basil's grave.

Lillian lived a long life and was finally laid to rest in the graveyard extension that had been the school garden, the very garden her youngest boy had tended to many years before.

The 5th Battalion Coldstream Guards suffered progressive losses in the nine months since landing in Normandy. Of the original battalion strength of approximately 850 men, a total of 228 of the officers and men had been killed. Many times more were wounded, totalling more than the original battalion strength. Many only lasted a few days, a few lucky ones survived the full nine months. It is not known how many later died of their wounds or disease like Basil, whilst on active service. They were raised at the time of our country's most desperate need. They all did their duty and fought bravely so that we can live in freedom from tyranny. Let us hope that the 5th Battalion will never be needed to be raised again. All of the boys have now stood down and are resting in peace together.

Basil's grave shortly after burial

*The War Memorial in
Cumnor village*

*The left side face bearing
Basil's name*

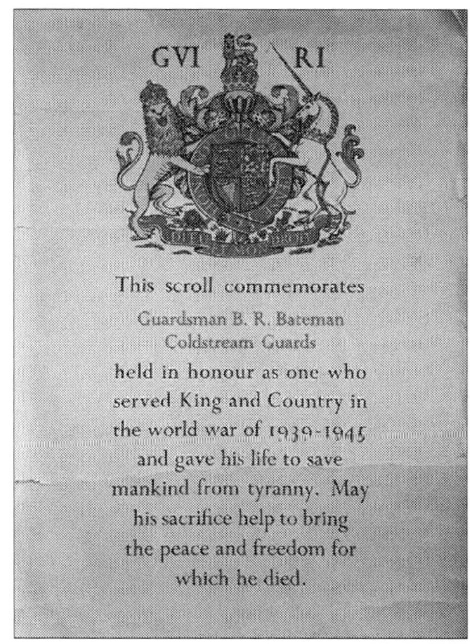

ADDENDUM I

Belsen Concentration Camp

Belsen was liberated on the 15th of April 1945. This humanitarian crisis created overwhelming logistical problems for the forces liberating it. The call went out for help from surrounding forces in the area and combat troops from many different units as well as medical units were called on to assist. The SS guards rounded up in the camp were forced at gunpoint by the combat troops to load the ragged skeletal corpses onto flatbed lorries, then drive them across the camp where they were unceremoniously carried or dragged to be thrown into the open mass graves. There is a large quantity of video footage available depicting this horrific nightmarish scene, but the many witness statements taken almost always say that the footage does not come close to the impact of the witnessing of this scene in person, or indeed the associated overwhelming stench.[1]

Basil's battalion war diary for the 15 – 16th April states: *'48 hours Maintenance and Rest in area of EMSTECK'*. Basil and the whole of the Guards Armoured Division were expecting a well-earned rest. Three days were promised and expected to be extended to one week. The German defence had softened as they were pulling back and preparing to defend Bremen. However, on the 17th of April the Guards Armoured Division (including Basil and the battalion) were taken over by XII Corps and ordered to advance 70 miles east to a *'holding area'* at Eilstorf, and attack and sever the autobahn between Bremen and Hamburg, whilst XXX Corps continued the attack towards Bremen. This seems a strange tactical decision given that they had been advancing towards Bremen since crossing the Rhine at Wesel and were within 30 miles of its south-western outskirts. Belsen is located at Bergen which is to the south-east of Bremen near Celle and not far from the 'holding area' at Eilstorf they were sent to. This huge deviation from their planned route must have been heavily influenced by the situation at Belsen and engineered to be in a position to provide support to the 11th Armoured Brigade at Belsen if needed.

Uncharacteristically, Basil's battalion war diary is lacking in detail during this period, in all other instances where there was significant planning it is detailed out meticulously. However, in this period there is no documentation of the decision making or of the significant logistics involved. This can be explained by the fact that the officer in charge of maintaining the war diary, Captain Pereira, was on an extended trip to Brussels from the 15th, not returning until the battalion were engaged in fighting near Neuenkirchen late in the day on the 18th when detailed recording continues. The war diary contains no mention of Belsen, but it does state that on the 18th of April the battalion drove from Eilstorf towards Visselhövede where they joined in with fighting there. The route they took from Eilstorf would have taken them within 20 miles of Belsen by road and considerably less if across open heathland.

Basil and 4 Company (and 1 Company) are not actually mentioned in the war diary from the 15th of April until the afternoon of the 19th, when the situation at Visselhövede required that 4 Company attack and capture Tewel. This leaves me with a quandary as the family story is that Basil guarded the German SS guards who were forced to bury the dead at Belsen. Given there is no mention in the war diary of this, and the lack of detailed recording during this period, pitted against the family story, it clearly requires investigation.

It is certainly possible that he and a contingent, or all of 4 Company, could have been sent on ahead as early as the 15th of April to Belsen. Another possibility is that they could have attended there on the 18th of April when the battalion were passing deliberately close to the Belsen camp, whilst the rest of the battalion continued towards Visselhövede.

The situation in Belsen is well documented as being chaotic and indeed the German SS guards were definitely forced to bury the dead under guard during that time frame. Manpower was desperately needed there and even though the fighting was continuing across the whole front line, the battalion had the capacity to offer urgently needed assistance there. The fact that they were allowed a rest period at Emstek was due to the fact that their front had quietened down as the Germans were retreating to the outskirts of Bremen to defend the city. There were numerous cases in other camps of combat troops, upon seeing the pitiful and horrific scenes, confronted by the unrepentant SS guards shot them out of hand. The Coldstream Guards and their inherent discipline would have been needed at this time.

Within a few days of its liberation the SS guards, disgusted with the task they were performing, and realising that prosecution and a death penalty was likely pending, slipped away at night, thus this 'guarding of them burying the dead' was within a time frame of only a few days between 16th and possibly 22nd April. Belsen was evacuated by the end of April and totally burned down by British troops due to Typhus infestation on 21st May.

Neither the Holocaust Museum in Washington, USA, nor the Imperial War Museum in London are able to confirm which combat troops actually attended Belsen in those first few days after liberation. It is known that many various troops did attend, as well as medical units and other allied units in the area who were merely sent there as witnesses to the horrific scene. Without documentary proof there is of course no way of confirming that Basil did enter Belsen Camp, but the salient facts are that:

- the whole of the Guards Armoured Division were unexpectedly directed towards the camp away from their long term plan of advance towards Bremen,
- the battalion could afford to deploy some of their guardsmen to assist at Belsen due to the lull in activity on their front,
- the unusual lack of detail in the war diary that fails to record events during the window of time when Basil could have been deployed to the camp,
- the fact that war diaries were then predominantly concerned with prosecuting the war effort only,

- the fact that there is no mention of Basil's 4 Company in the war diary from the 15th until the 19th of April even though the battalion were in contact with the enemy,
- the urgent humanitarian crisis presented to the liberating troops with the associated call for urgent assistance,
- the need at the camp for the discipline the Coldstream Guards are famous for,
- there were many other undocumented combat troops from other units in the area who entered Belsen shortly after its liberation,
- the documented and filmed evidence of the SS guards burying the dead whilst being guarded by fighting troops,
- the strong family story that Basil guarded SS guards whilst they buried the dead,

Using the civil law legal term *'on the balance of probability'* the evidence suggests that he did enter the camp and guard the SS guards whilst burying the dead on the 18th of April, and highly likely that he was at the camp from as early as the 16th of April, returning to the battalion's location near Tewel on the afternoon of the 19th of April 1945.

Finally there is a post by user-name 'polcirkel' on the *BBC – WW2 People's War webpage* which states that his father was a tank driver in the Coldstream Guards and had informed him that he had entered Belsen and had described the horrific scenes there. He claimed to have been filmed using a bulldozer to bury the bodies. This webpage is now closed and not possible to authenticate this story but it does suggest that some of the 1st Battalion Coldstream Guards tanks, who were paired with the 5ᵗʰ Battalion, may also have entered Belsen.

Note

1   The Imperial War Museum have multiple photographs in their collection of the horrors in Belsen Concentration Camp. One example being Ref. no. – BU4025 which shows British troops guarding the German guards whilst they load emaciated bodies onto a flatbed lorry.

ADDENDUM II

Cause of death

Basil was diagnosed with pyelitis within eighteen days of his death. A urinary tract or bladder infection is usually responsible for pyelitis and is generally caught from the bacteria in faeces. If it goes unnoticed or does not receive proper treatment, bacteria can spread to the renal pelvis. This is known as a complicated bladder infection. Acute pyelitis is characterised by a general feeling of sickness, pain in the area of the kidneys, burning when urinating as well as a high fever and shivering. In 1945, pyelitis was diagnosed on the basis of the patient's medical history, the symptoms, and with a blood and urine examination. In severe cases it can lead to kidney failure. If a backup of urine occurs then this can lead to sepsis (blood poisoning) which can be fatal.

As Basil was still in the military at the time of his death, I had assumed that the 'army form B' notification acted as the death certificate, but I later discovered a civil death certificate listing the primary and secondary causes of death in the conventional way. It confirmed tubercular kidney (renal tuberculosis) but indicates that a full autopsy must have taken place as it also identifies miliary tuberculosis, which is grain sized particles evident in the lungs. The primary cause of death is recorded as uraemia, which is a raised level of toxic waste compounds in the blood caused by kidney failure.

Tuberculosis (TB) is an airborne disease caused by a type of bacterium called mycobacterium tuberculosis. Until modern times tuberculosis was a prolific killer. It can be caught by breathing in the air that an infected person has contaminated. The symptoms depend on which part of the body is affected. Tuberculosis usually develops slowly, and it may take several years before illness is noticed. Symptoms may not begin until months or even years after initial infection, in some cases no symptoms at all. Only around 10% of people go on to develop the full disease. It is not fully understood why the infection reactivates but it is known that it is more likely with impaired immune systems. Amongst other factors, extreme stress and infection are known to impair the immune system. Other conditions that make a reactivation more likely include chronic kidney problems (such as that caused by pyelitis), diabetes, cancer, and smoking. General symptoms are lack of appetite and weight loss, high temperature, night sweats, extreme tiredness or fatigue. If lungs are affected – then coughing, and breathlessness. If the bladder or kidney is affected, usually when the immune system is weak, then this is referred to as renal tuberculosis.

Additional symptoms of renal tuberculosis include pain when urinating; headaches, back, flank, or abdominal pain; and blood in urine. Renal tuberculosis may also be caused by other variants including mycobacterium bovis, a slow-growing bacterium and the causative agent of tuberculosis in cattle (known as bovine tuberculosis). Most people are at very low risk of being infected, those at higher risk include individuals who work with cattle, such as dairy farming. Bovine tuberculosis can be spread directly from person to person when people with the disease in their lungs cough or sneeze.

It is possible that Basil caught tuberculosis from an early age, or possibly at fourteen years old when working on the farm with the resident dairy herd. Today tuberculosis in cattle is controlled, all milk is pasteurised, and the risk of contracting bovine tuberculosis is very low. This was far from the case prior to the 1960s when there was only voluntary testing of cattle by farmers who in general expressed an unwillingness to stamp out bovine tuberculosis, largely driven by financial reasons. Estimates of the number of tuberculous cattle ranged from 25 to 40 per cent of the national herd.

Basil was clearly unwell when he returned home on leave on 16th of December 1945. He mentions in his letter home on 12th December 1945 that he got very cold during a parade. This was a likely symptom of his illness. In an earlier letter dated 9th December 1945 he mentions that he "is in the best of health". Could this have been the opposite, him reassuring a worried mother that she had nothing to worry about him? One of his friends, George Davidson, mentions in a letter after his death that he knew that Basil had been ill for some time. There is then, some evidence that he was ill some time prior to coming home on the 16th of December. The 5th Battalion was officially ended on 31st October 1945 forcing his transfer to the 1st Battalion and a change of location. This period must have caused considerable upheaval to the infrastructure of the guards. A soldier complaining of sickness may well have gained very little sympathy and help at that time.

In summary, his cause of death is without doubt related to him contracting tuberculosis at some earlier time in his life. There it lay dormant until possibly reactivated by him contracting pyelitis that lowered his immune system and caused trauma to his kidneys, or perhaps by low immunity caused by the extreme stress of battle, and heavy smoking. Symptoms of pyelitis must have been apparent for that interim diagnosis to have been made. It is certainly possible that he could have caught pyelitis from bacteria within the extreme insanitary conditions of Belsen or indeed at any time whilst he was on active service, leading to severe kidney trauma. He experienced almost non-stop combat from February to May 1945. Without doubt this must have caused stress way beyond that which would be experienced by anyone in peace time and certainly a potential cause of reactivation of the infection.

Specialist tuberculosis treatment was available at Shaftesbury Military Hospital The principal treatment for tuberculosis was exposure to sunlight and fresh air, until successful tests with the newly discovered 'Streptomycin' in USA in 1944/45 led to it being made available in Britain towards the end of 1946 sadly just too late for Basil.

ADDENDUM III

Citations and Reports

The Attack on the Siegfried Line at Müll on the
16th of February 1945

Citations for Medals awarded for Bravery relating to the
attack:

<u>No. 3861848 LANCE-SERGEANT WILFRED CLITHEROE
– 4 Company</u>

*On 16th February, 1945, this N.C.O. was commanding a
section in the left-hand platoon of the left forward company
in the Battalion attack on the German defences south
of Hommersum. His platoon's objective was some farm
buildings on the far side of a flooded stream which could only
be approached by a causeway about fifty yards long through
flood water. The bridge crossing the stream itself had been
blown, leaving a gap 15 feet wide, crossed only now with
lengths of light railway line. The causeway and bridge were
covered by automatic fire from the farm on the far side, and the
platoon plan was to support the crossing by the 2-inch mortar.*

However, without waiting for this fire to become effective or even for the final order to go, this Non-Commissioned Officer (N.C.O.) led his section with great dash straight along the causeway, over the partially demolished bridge and into the farm buildings from which at this moment the enemy fled. Throughout the whole attack Lance-Sergeant Clitheroe's leadership and example were a great encouragement to the whole platoon.

<u>No. 2658364 CORPORAL (LANCE-SERGEANT) VICTOR RUDDICK [VERNON FOREST RUDDICK] – 3 Company</u>
Throughout the whole campaign in North-West Europe this N.C.O. has been one of the outstanding section leaders in the Battalion and one of the few to come through all the fighting unscathed. After each of our many battles his name has been brought to my notice for outstanding bravery and devotion to duty. A typical example occurred on the 16th February, 1945, when his section was the leading one in his company, which on that day passed through the original forward companies in the attack on the strongly defended German defences at Müll, south-east of Gennep. The platoon objective was a farm 300 yards beyond the main German anti-tank obstacle, and having crossed this Lance-Sergeant Ruddick led his section for 300 yards over open country in the face of the fire from at least two German machine guns. On reaching the farm he approached a door and fired his Sten into the house. The gun jammed and after throwing a grenade he rushed in, wounding two Germans and capturing ten more. This is merely a typical example of this N.C.O.'s dash and initiative, which have at all times been of the utmost encouragement to the rest of his platoon and indeed to the whole company.

<u>No. 14402668 GUARDSMAN ROBERT GREIG –
1 Company</u>

On 16th February, 1945, Guardsman Greig was a member of the right-hand section of the right-hand company of the Battalion attack on the German defences south of Hommersum. After a long advance under heavy enemy artillery fire, this section was within a few hundred yards of its final objective when it was temporarily unsighted by a smoke screen put down for the benefit of the formation on the right. For this reason they did not see a German machine-gun post in their vicinity until it had opened up at short range, killing the section commander and one other man. Guardsman Greig at once assumed command of the section and seized the Bren gun, but while he was doing this two more men in the section had been killed by the same German machine-gun post. Guardsman Greig, now single-handed, charged the enemy post, killed the two men on the machine gun and put the remainder to flight. He then fell, wounded in four places in the leg. As a result of his fine action he allowed the few remaining men of the section to continue their advance, thus covering the right flank of his platoon and, incidentally, of the whole company.

<u>No. 2660552 GUARDSMAN (U./LANCE-CORPORAL)
HECTOR ROBERTSON DODDS, M.M.</u>

This N.C.O. was in charge of the stretcher-bearers attached to a rifle company in his battalion throughout the whole campaign and during that time there is no doubt that, thanks to his utter disregard for his own safety and very high sense of devotion to duty, he saved the lives of many of his comrades and lessened the suffering of many others. Of the many cases possible to cite for outstanding bravery two must suffice as illustrations.

During his company's attack against the Siegfried Line at Müll on 16th February, 1945, his headquarters received a direct hit from a shell which wounded two of the stretcher-bearers and badly shook this N.C.O. However, he at once rendered first aid to his companions and then proceeded to the right forward platoon, who had just suffered the loss of one complete section by enemy medium machine-gun fire. Corporal Dodds had to cross this hostile fire himself before he could reach the wounded men and this he did without the slightest hesitation. On arrival a heavy smoke concentration was put down on to his platoon locality, but despite all this Corporal Dodds continued moving from man to man until all had been dealt with.........

W.S./ Lieutenant ERIK RICHARD SIDNEY FIFOOT This officer has been an outstanding patrol and platoon leader ever since joining the Battalion in August, 1944. Every time he has had the opportunity to distinguish himself for bravery and devotion to duty he has done so. Outstanding examples occurred twice during Operation "Veritable." In the battalion attack on Müll, south-east of Gennep, he commanded the right-hand forward platoon which had to cross 3,000 yards of open country in face of heavy and accurate enemy D.F. fire and considerable small-arms fire from farmhouses and concrete "haystacks." Over all of this distance this officer's fine example was of the utmost encouragement and resulted, despite heavy casualties, in complete victory............

The 'Brussels Sprout' was the Battalion's Newsletter and was periodically passed out to the men in the battalion. Edition Number 13 was passed out to the men two days after the attack.

THE BRUSSELS SPROUT
NO. 13
Sunday, 18th February, 1945

MESSAGE FROM THE COMMANDING OFFICER.

I wish to congratulate everyone on their performance on the 16th, and by everyone I mean exactly that; not only the Company, Platoon and Section Commanders but every Guardsman who advanced without hesitation to final objective through the heavy enemy defensive fire.

The Brigadier has asked me to send you all his congratulations and those of our Divisional Commander who watched the whole attack from some high ground.

Also the Commander of the Division with which we were then operating most kindly found time yesterday to visit us in order to send you his congratulations and thanks "for having fought such a fine battle".

The secret of your success lay in each man's determination to get on regardless of cost and the result is a force which no German action has yet been able to stop or will be able to, until the fighting is over and may that day now be not long delayed.

HOW THE BATTLE WENT.

The Battalion's attack the day before yesterday was the first item of a very considerable programme of attacks, and the list of operations handed to us just before the battle had resembled a menu for an eight course dinner and was a most imposing affair with ourselves heading the list.

There has been a certain amount of argument as to whether the attack ought to be called after the village of Müll which we captured just across the German frontier or referred to as breaching the SIEGFRIED LINE, which we are also quite entitled to claim. My purely personal view is that Müll is the first village on GERMAN soil captured by a COLDSTREAM Battalion for a great many years and is therefore of more significance than the SIEGFRIED LINE which a great many people have operated against and in the British sector is a very bogus affair compared with what the Americans dealt with near AACHEN.

The SIEGFRIED LINE proper ends at MUNCHEN GLADBACH and from here northwards the German defences are only a hastily made extension mostly constructed by conscript civilian labour; nonetheless in case people at a future date argue that there was nothing here at all it would be perhaps a good thing to give a rough outline of the actual defences we encountered.

In front of the line several mock haystacks were spread across the countryside, camouflaged extremely well with straw so as to be quite undistinguishable for the article they were, actually thick concrete casements built to hold a section and complete with a store for heating and cooking purposes.

No. 4 Company who led the attack on the right (later corrected to 'left') and overran several of them report that happily none were actually occupied during the attack. Next came a more or less continuous trench which ran from the overflowed dyke on our right southwards. A very ineffective affair presumably made for intercommunication and cover between the groups of farm buildings from which the enemy actually fought. It was certainly not used to fight from and does not seem to have been of any value though it must have taken a lot of labour to construct. Finally there was an 8 yard wide Anti-Tank ditch, a genuine enough obstacle, though in practise the ground everywhere was so boggy as to prove a complete obstacle to our supporting tanks the minute they left the far from firm going provided by the roads and tracks.

The defenders were all from 122nd Grenadier Regiment and though they fought a lot better than Battalion Riegel's whom we met the day before they were not up to the standards of six months ago and we had more casualties from the considerable defensive Artillery fire that the enemy put down than from the enemy infantry.

No. 4 Company forced their way over the floods via a very doubtful causeway and also over the Anti-Tank ditch both of which were under fire at the time, without a single casualty.

The most stubborn defence was met by No. 1 Company in the area of a small bridge over the Anti-Tank ditch that was in their area. The enemy were very strongly placed here and were at one moment reported to be forming up for a counterattack, so No. 1 Company were ordered to call off the attacks on it. However heavy stinks were put down in this area and nothing come of any threat that was impending.

After No. 4 and No. 1 Companies reached their objectives No. 3 Company passed through over the Anti-Tank ditch and captured STARTENHOF and RETUT. Actually the closely strung groups of farm buildings made much further and wider mopping up actions necessary which they successfully accomplished.

Darkness was coming on towards the end of things, the enemy Artillery action died down, and as we have since discovered the bulk of the enemy withdrew to SIEBENGEWALD leaving only a few snipers behind, and the WELSH GUARDS captured HASSUM at four in the morning without meeting opposition.

An unusual enemy weapon was reported by No. 2 Company and their description of the incident is corroborated by the IRISH GUARDS. Whatever the shell or rocket used by the enemy was, in this case half a dozen landed without any preliminary warning whistle, and the blast and crater made by this unknown weapon was reported to be very considerable. No explanation of this has yet been found and any further information would be gratefully received, particularly bits of whatever it was that came down.

The final count of prisoners came to 152 Other Ranks and two Officers, which with the exception of ARRAS and the days of the "Great Swan" when we got over 3,000 is about our third best bag. (BOURG LEOPOLD operations were the best total). In addition numerous Machine Guns, Faustpatroners, Panzerschreck and an Anti-Tank gun were captured.

General RENNIE General Officer Commanding 51 DIVISION visited Battalion H.Q. next day and thanked the Commanding Officer for the very successful part of the day's Operations that the Battalion had accomplished.

As a prelude to the end of the German Army this side of the RHINE we can be most satisfied with the part we have played, and as the battle leaves us behind on either flank and advances towards GOCH the past few days will stand us as a very good precedent for whatever our next task in this phase of ending the war may be.

Citations from Bravery Medals won during the attack on Metzekath on the 5th of March 1945

LIEUTENANT MICHAEL WALL – 4 Company
Military Medal

On the 5th of March 1945 this Officer was commanding one of the forward platoons in the battalion attack on Metzekath on the Bonninghardt Ridge. The line of advance of the platoon was up a road through some Woods which came to an end before reaching the objective. On reaching the edge of this wood the platoon came under heavy fire from a 75mm Anti Tank Gun, small arms fire and bazooka fire from a house farther on. At this moment the platoon mortar Corporal was killed by a direct hit from the Anti Tank Gun but Lieutenant Wall managed to get a smokescreen put down by his two inch mortar to cover his advance across the open while he led one section to assault the gun. The assault was successful despite the fact that the gun crew fought to the last, the leader being bayoneted in the act of reloading the gun. Lieutenant Wall then led on to attack the house whence the small arms fire came and which was equally stubbornly held, every German having to be killed and none surrendering. Lieutenant Wall then led on to his final objective now for the first time taking prisoners as he went. Throughout the whole attack this officer showed the greatest dash and leadership. His conduct was an inspiration to his platoon and there is no doubt that they would follow him anywhere as they have done from Normandy to the Rhine. There is no doubt that it was largely thanks to this Officer's great bravery and power of leadership that his Company attack was able to keep up its momentum and thus the battalion attack to be entirely successful in time for consolidation to be carried out before darkness fell.

No. 2662917 CORPORAL (LANCE-SERGEANT) JOHN LINDSEY – 4 Company

On the 5th March, 1945, this N.C.O. was commanding one of the forward sections in the Battalion attack on Metzekath in the Bonninghardt. The line of advance of the platoon was up a road through some woods which came to an end before reaching the objective. On coming to the edge of the woods the platoon came under fire from a 75-mm. anti-tank gun, small-arms fire and bazooka fire from a house. This N.C.O. was ordered to give covering fire while his platoon commander led the other sections in an assault on the anti-tank gun. Appreciating that the assaulting party would come under heavy fire from the house while assaulting the gun, Lance-Sergeant Lindsey on his own initiative led his section across the bullet-swept ground and attacked the house under very heavy fire. He fought his way in with grenades, being twice blown off his feet by blast from bazooka bombs while doing so. Undeterred, he led his section on, killing two of the enemy and putting the rest to flight. He then led his section in pursuit, capturing them all to the number of thirteen. This action had the effect of helping the platoon attack to be successful, and Lance-Sergeant Lindsey at once pushed on with the rest of the platoon to the final objective and ordered his section to dig in. He then collapsed from the effects of the blast of the bazooka bombs. This N.C.O. has taken part in every attack since the Normandy days, and this latest example of utter disregard for this own safety and complete devotion to duty is typical of his exemplary conduct during the whole campaign. There is no doubt that his great gallantry on the 5th March, 1945, was largely responsible for the complete success of the Battalion attack.

No. 2661863 ACTING SERGEANT CHARLES HANDLEY – 3 Company

At the beginning of Operation "Veritable" this N.C.O. was platoon sergeant of a platoon. On the 5th March, 1945, prior to the Battalion attack on Metzekath, the forward companies, which included his, were unfortunately heavily shelled on the start line. This N.C.O's platoon commander and a quarter of the platoon strength were killed or wounded at that time, but Sergeant Handley immediately rallied the survivors and, despite this unfavourable start and due to his outstanding leadership, he led them forward to fulfil the mission allotted to them in every respect and despite stubborn enemy opposition...

Citations for Bravery won during the attack on the Wesel bridgehead at Haus Loo on the 9th of March 1945

W.S./ Lieutenant ERIK RICHARD SIDNEY FIFOOT – 1 Company

This officer has been an outstanding patrol and platoon leader ever since joining the Battalion in August, 1944. Every time he has had the opportunity to distinguish himself for bravery and devotion to duty he has done so. Outstanding examples occurred twice during Operation "Veritable."...

....On the 9th March this officer was commanding a forward platoon in the Battalion attack on the Wesel bridgehead. His platoon started to suffer casualties before crossing the start line, and on reaching that they were met with further heavy small-arms and mortar fire.

Despite all this, Lieutenant Fifoot led his platoon with conspicuous dash and gallantry. No sooner was the original objective reached than he was ordered to carry out a difficult manoeuvre to the flank to meet a threatened German counterattack. Despite the intense and accurate mortar and nebelwerfer fire, he accomplished this manoeuvre with great skill, thus neutralizing the threat to his company's whole position...

W.S./ Lieutenant The Hon. PETER ALGERNON STRUTT – 2 Company

This officer started by commanding the reserve platoon of a forward company in the Battalion's attack on to the Xanten-Rheinberg Road on 9th March, 1945. Early in the battle the two forward platoons were held up by extremely heavy machine-gun fire from the right flank. They were in the open and suffering heavy casualties. When he was ordered to advance round the left flank, this officer led his platoon with great skill and dash and, clearing the ground in front, led his platoon on to their most forward objective. At this stage the company commander was wounded and most of the company headquarters knocked out. This officer then took charge of the company and under intense fire from both small arms and heavy weapons organized and sited the consolidation positions. He saw to the evacuation of the wounded and personally directed fire on to the enemy who were in close contact. Throughout the battle the fine example and courage shown by this officer were an inspiration to his company and one of the main factors in the success of the operation.

Temporary Major DAVID ARTHUR KENNARD –
1 Company

On the 9th March, 1945, this officer commanded the left forward company in the Battalion attack on the Xanten – Rheinberg road which resulted in the clearing up of the Wesel bridgehead. His company came under heavy mortar and artillery fire in the F.U.P. and as soon as they crossed the start line under aimed small-arms fire as well. Before the operation started it was doubted if the final objective could ever be reached, but without hesitation this officer led his company forward to it and, despite loss, consolidated in the fact of very heavy and accurate mortar and nebelwerfer fire. Once there his position was threatened not only from the front but also from his open left flank. He immediately altered his dispositions to meet the new threat and, despite everything the enemy could do, remained on his objective until the enemy wearied of assaulting him.

There is no doubt that a large share of the credit for this completely successful operation must be given to the intrepid leadership displayed throughout by Major Kennard and his masterly handling of his company during the advance and subsequent consolidation. His personal example was an inspiration to all ranks, and his power of command and leadership of the very highest order.

No. 2661863 ACTING SERGEANT CHARLES HANDLEY
– 3 Company

On the 9th March, Sergeant Handley was commanding the platoon in the Battalion attack on the Wesel bridgehead. This time his company was in reserve, but as the forward companies had been ordered to bypass as much opposition as possible in order to reach their objective much bitter hand-to-hand fighting fell to the lot of the platoon before the area allotted to them as their objective was clear of enemy. During the whole period this N.C.O. displayed the utmost gallantry and dash in leading assaults on house after house, all of which were occupied by the enemy and defended by them to the last. Throughout the whole period under review, until he was himself wounded in the Battalion attack over the River Haze, whether as platoon sergeant or platoon commander, his example has been an inspiration to the whole platoon and has undoubtedly been a great factor in the proud record of this N.C.O.'s company.

No. 2663989 CORPORAL (LANCE-SERGEANT) DENNIS FRANK JORDAN – 2 Company

On 9th March, 1945, the Battalion was ordered to capture the Xanten-Rheinberg Road. Extremely heavy machine-gun fire was met by the right-hand leading sections as soon as they crossed the start line, and they suffered heavy casualties, yet this N.C.O., who was commanding one of them, showed outstanding courage and skill in fighting his way forward. At one time he took on a German section single-handed and liquidated it, although he was under fire from paratroopers in adjacent houses. It was largely due to this N.C.O.'s leadership and dash that the company was able to fight its way to its objective. On consolidation Lance-Sergeant Jordan had to take over command of his platoon and although under continuous fire from snipers and Spandaus he went round and personally sited the sections and helped them to reorganize.

This N.C.O. has in previous battles shown a similar complete disregard for his own personal safety and his example has been an inspiration to the company.

No. 2660552 GUARDSMAN (U./LANCE-CORPORAL) HECTOR ROBERTSON DODDS, M.M.

This N.C.O. was in charge of the stretcher-bearers attached to a rifle company in his battalion throughout the whole campaign and during that time there is no doubt that, thanks to his utter disregard for his own safety and very high sense of devotion to duty, he saved the lives of many of his comrades and lessened the suffering of many others. Of the many cases possible to cite for outstanding bravery two must suffice as illustrations....

Apart from these exploits on behalf of his own company the opportunity twice came for him to help the men of other regiments, and on both occasions his action was gratefully brought to my notice by the commanding officers concerned.

The first occasion was ... the second time was on the 9th March, 1945, when the SCOTS GUARDS began the assault on the Wesel bridgehead when their centre line was cut and their R.A.P. staff separated from their forward companies. This corporal did all that could be done to make good their loss.

Report on the advance from Ems to Boen from the 3rd – 11th April 1945

EMS TO BOEN.

Superficially our progress from the EMS to BOEN has been disappointingly slow, but in view of the enemy situation, it is hardly surprising that we have been unable to achieve a break-through and the import and of last week is not measured in miles but in damage done to the Para Army whose numbers we have been steadily reducing day by day, which is the only way they can be dealt with since there is very little hope that they will ever surrender as a formation. It would have been more spectacular and less costly to swan across GERMANY in the old manner, but there is a job that has to be done one day and we can now claim to have played our share.

Starting off from a river, after the delays caused by bridging and the time this gives the enemy to get organised, is always difficult and leaving the EMS was no exception. The SCOTS/ WELSH Group abandoned the right Centre Line after the first two miles and moved on the left hand one, and, in order to open up as many possibilities as the roads would allow, we were ordered to continue on their old route from LINGEN to RAMSEL late that afternoon. Thanks to the efforts of No. 1 Company and No. 1 Squadron, by nightfall we had got RAMSEL and BAKUM and next morning were able to start very nearly level with the SCOTS/WELSH Group.

It was known that the line LENGERICH THUINE would be held and a rapid barrage down the road together with Typhoon attacks on the village was laid on in advance. Surprisingly THUINE was held only by a bewildered Company of 104 P.G.R. and we were masters of the place with comparatively little difficulty. LENGERICH however, proved to be the local point through which all the forces of 7 Para Division were withdrawing, so that instead of peacefully following the SCOTS/ WELSH Group through the town while 5 BRIGADE proceeded down the route we opened up at THUINE, we found that the SCOTS/WELSH Group were unable to get LENGERICH and we had to do something about it.

The 1st Battalion Recce Troop successfully discovered a route round LENGERICH and looking rather apprehensively to our right and left we succeeded in infiltrating our way between the strong point of LENGERICH to the North and another strong point in the woods to the South to emerge on the main road behind LENGERICH, a manoeuvre which appears to have bolted the enemy for it was soon afterward found that LENGERICH had been evacuated and the WELSH GUARDS tanks came down the road to meet us.

We led off the next day full of hope, but by evening had not gone far. There was a heavy stink on our Start Point, defended road blocks in every village and a number of S.Ps that continued to harass the column from head to tail throughout the day. By midday we were up to BERGE which it was appreciated would be a tough nut to crack and as a preliminary, Typhoons were sent in against it. A Squadron of tanks tried to rush the town from the South but several were knocked out by an Anti-Tank gun and Bazooka men who abounded in every house. No. 4 Company then took on the clearing, and after dealing with an exceptionally stubborn pocket in the North end of BERGE, No. 1 Company passed through them and captured the group of farmsteads about a mile beyond. From here the SCOTS/ WELSH Group took the lead and covered the next ten miles up to MENSLAGE, notable for the fact that they had to cross four canals all with their bridges blown, a bad headache for the ROYAL ENGINEERS, and ahead of them the River HASE.

The HASE was our task and though we got up to it unopposed, within a very short while it became obvious that the rest of the job was not going to be so easy and peering over the bank at the Germans thickly lining the opposite bank 100 yards away did little to reassure one. Here No. 4 Company pulled off a great coup and captured a bridge, or rather a bit of a bridge, about four miles upstream. A difficult operation but it saved us from boating across and undoubtedly saved a number of lives. Even at this stage it was far from plain sailing, as the *defenders of the bridge fought on further back and there was danger that the Battalion would become too deeply involved in getting up to BOEN through the woods to be able to put in an attack, however 3 Company pushed their way through and all was well. No. 3 Company and No. 1 Company then cleared the village and No. 2 Company cleared the river bank, which was probably the most difficult job as despite the fact that their positions were being taken from behind, the numerous enemy we had surveyed from the other side in the morning, turned about and were just as stubborn with the river behind them as in front of them.*

Since we crossed the RHINE we have taken over 700 Prisoners of War, exact details will be given when there is time to work them out.

Citations for Bravery during capture of the bridge over the River Ems at Lingen on the 3rd April 1945

CAPTAIN IAN LIDDELL VICTORIA CROSS – 3 Company

"In Germany on 3rd April, 1945, Captain Liddell was commanding a Company of the Coldstream Guards, which was ordered to capture intact a bridge over the River Ems near Lingen. The bridge was covered on the far bank by an enemy strong point, which was subsequently discovered to consist of 150 entrenched infantry supported by three 88 mm. and two 20 mm. guns. The bridge was also prepared for demolition with 500 Ib. bombs which could plainly be seen. Having directed his two leading platoons on to the near bank,

Captain Liddell ran forward alone to the bridge and scaled the 10 feet high road block guarding it, with the intention of neutralising the charges and taking the bridge intact. In order to achieve his object he had to cross the whole length of the bridge by himself under intense enemy fire, which increased as his object became apparent to the Germans. Having disconnected the charges on the far side, he re-crossed the bridge and cut the wires on the near side. It was necessary for him to kneel forming an easy target whilst he successively cut the wires. He then discovered that there were also charges underneath the bridge and completely undeterred he also disconnected these. His task completed he then climbed up on to the road block in full view of the enemy and signalled his leading platoon to advance. Thus alone and unprotected, without cover and under heavy enemy fire, he achieved his object. The bridge was captured intact and the way cleared to the advance across the river Ems. His outstanding gallantry and superb example of courage will never be forgotten by those who saw it. This very brave officer has since died of wounds subsequently received in action."

No. 2664442 LANCE-CORPORAL JOHN EDWARD WILLIAM ROYAL – 3 Company

On 3rd April, 1945, this N.C.O. was commanding the section which led the assault on the bridge over the River Ems at Altenlingen. After the dash across the bridge, in the face of heavy fire from 88's and small arms, the section fought its way into a deep trench, but were held up at a bend by a party of enemy round the corner. Heavy enemy fire was sweeping the top of the trench from one direction, and our own supporting fire from our tanks from the other, but despite all this Lance-

Corporal Royal, without any hesitation, climbed out into the open and ran along the top of the trench for over eighty yards firing his Sten gun at the enemy in the trench who were holding up the advance of his action. Some he accounted for, some surrendered and the remainder who fled were killed by fire from the tanks.

This action enabled the platoon to complete the clearing of the trench and ensured that the bridge was captured intact.

There is no doubt that the absolute disregard of his own personal safety shown by this N.C.O. was responsible for the speedy elimination of enemy resistance on the far bank and the completion of the whole operation with such dash and determination that the enemy was never given a chance to reorganize his defence.

Citations for Bravery during capture of the Barracks at Lingen on the 4th of April 1945

No. 2662048 SERGEANT NORMAN DUCKWORTH

On 4th April 1945, Sergeant Duckworth was the platoon sergeant of a forward platoon in the company of the Coldstream Guards detailed to attack the large barracks west of Lingen. The attack went in at last light and the tank support was unable to keep up with the infantry owing to a stream. In the circumstances the clearing of the barrack buildings became a matter of great difficulty and smoke had to be used to get the sections across the gaps between, as all were covered by Spandau fire. In this instance the forward sections were across, but when the remaining one attempted to follow, the section leader was killed and the section paused. At once this N.C.O. ran back to them without any smoke protection, rallied them, and brought them across the gap. With this extra support the pillbox which was holding up the platoon was captured and the advance continued. One hundred and forty-two prisoners were taken by the company.

This N.C.O.'s unhesitating acceptance of all risks and great power of leadership (which has been invaluable to the platoon ever since Normandy) undoubtedly resulted in keeping up the impetus of the attack and the entirely successful completion of the task.

Citations for Bravery during the attack on Boen and River Haze Crossing on the 11th April 1945

W.S./ CAPTAIN (TEMPORARY MAJOR) JOHN D'HENIN HAMILTON – 4 Company

On 11th April, 1945, the Battalion was ordered to force a crossing of the River Haze and establish a bridgehead at Boen, using boat equipment. The map, however, disclosed a small bridge two miles to the east and Major Hamilton was ordered to take his company with one troop of tanks under command to investigate this bridge and, if possible, seize it. On arrival the bridge was found to be partially blown and strongly defended on the far bank. Major Hamilton at once organized the best available fire plan and then personally led a platoon over the broken bridge in the face of accurate and heavy small-arms fire. Such dash and determination upset the defenders, who numbered about 150, and who were all either killed or captured or withdrew to a small village about 500 yards to the north. Without a pause, Major Hamilton followed them up, appreciating that he must clear the village too in order to make the bridge safe for the rest of the Battalion to use.

As a result of this action the whole Battalion (less any wheels) crossed the Haze before the enemy completed the destruction of the bridge by shell fire, and the subsequent attack on Boen was carried out with much less loss of life and time than would otherwise have been the case.

This was achieved by the outstanding power of leadership and personal bravery of Major Hamilton.

W.S./CAPTAIN (TEMPORARY MAJOR) *The Hon.* DIGBY MICHAEL GODFREY JOHN WILLOUGHBY –
2 Company

On 11th April 1945, this officer was commander of his company in the Battalion attack to gain a crossing of the River Haze. Owing to the forcing of a bridge, at the last moment the whole plan was changed and the role allotted to the company was to sweep south of the village of Boen and clear the north bank of the river, not then thought to be any longer strongly held. The bulk of the supporting fire, therefore, was directed on to the village itself and beyond. From the time the company debouched into the open it became obvious that all the objectives allotted to it were strongly held by a numerous enemy garrison who were able to shoot at it from front, flank and rear. Major Willoughby, with vigour and determination, directed his forward platoons on despite loss and then went himself to his reserve platoon, commanded by a sergeant, and personally directed its operation against the most troublesome enemy positions. As a result, over forty members of the 61st Parachute Regiment were then killed or captured and the whole situation softened up so that all the company objectives were soon afterwards seized. Undoubtedly it was this officer's great gallantry and outstanding leadership which were responsible for the successful completion of the operation. Major Willoughby has commanded his company in every action fought by the Battalion from Normandy onwards, except one, and has always been outstanding, but on this occasion the special circumstances conspired to give him his opportunity to excel.

No. 2660552 GUARDSMAN (U./LANCE-CORPORAL) HECTOR ROBERTSON DODDS, M.M.

This N.C.O. was in charge of the stretcher-bearers attached to a rifle company in his battalion throughout the whole campaign and during that time there is no doubt that, thanks to his utter disregard for his own safety and very high sense of devotion to duty, he saved the lives of many of his comrades and lessened the suffering of many others. Of the many cases possible to cite for outstanding bravery two must suffice as illustrations.

On 11th April, 1945, this N.C.O.'s company were lining the bank of the River Haze prior to forcing a crossing at another place. The company were under heavy and accurate small-arms fire, and movement appeared impossible. Casualties were being suffered and each time the call came for stretcher-bearers this N.C.O. went without any hesitation and amidst a hail of bullets from at least two enemy medium machine guns from across the river.

A report on progress during the last few days of the war – 'Brussels Sprout' Saturday the 14th of April 1945

'A RESUME OF EVENTS.

Looking at the war as a whole it is hard to find any reason why it continues, except the intense stupidity of the German Nation, and the fear that if they surrender reprisals will be taken against their families.

The defence of the North of GERMANY, and in particular between the WESER and the ELBE was arranged personally by HIMMLER, and from the news it appears that he is himself either in DENMARK or along the northern coast and probably still in control of a more or less coherent command.

In so far as there is a purpose in the Germans still holding out, our battles are still the battle for BREMEN and HAMBURG, as until the ground between the ELBE and the WESER has been mopped up and the two estuaries are in our control, we cannot use either of these ports, both of which are of vital importance to us.

Our part in the operation has been mainly a series of town storming battles, and the catalogue of names is by now too long to go into in detail, NEUNKIRCHEN, then down on to the other centre line to capture the troublesome VISSELHOVEDE, up our own centre line once more, and SCHESSEL was added to the list, No. 1 Company and the tanks being led in by a willing Burgomaster. ROTTENBURG despite a lot of negotiations and a shower of propaganda, announced the they would hold on to the last man and last round. Fortunately the troops were not in agreement with this and over 700 Prisoners of War were captured which so upset the German Commander (also captured) that he committed suicide.

After ROTENBURG came ZEVEN which was perhaps the toughest of them, our troubles being added to by the fact that the enemy had a number of guns and apparently ample ammunition for its defence. The 1st Battalion captured a Mortar Bomb factory nearby.

Pushing West from ZEVEN we were only in the lead when we captured WENTEL, which was unopposed except for shelling, and in this sector the enemy have now entered behind the network of canals and waterways called the OSTE-HAMME Canal, which it is fortunately someone else's job to tackle.

We have now done a big switch-over to the other side of things. Yesterday's advance brought us to within five miles of STADE on the ELBER, which is of importance as there is one of the few remaining ferry systems across the river still in action here. The roads are now all cut, but news from the other Group suggest that the town is held.

It is becoming increasingly difficult to catalogue the kinds and number of Prisoners of War that we are getting in, but our total since crossing the WESER is over 500 and if wounded are counted as well, another 2,000 can be added, the inmates of the big hospitals in ROTENBURG and SCHEESSEL. Russians, Poles, Dutch, French, and innumerable other Prisoners of War and slave workers liberated runs to wholly astronomical figures that it is hard even to guess at. The GRENADIER Group who have liberated the concentration camp at SANDBOSTEL found 35,000 people there, most of them starving and with a Typhus epidemic.'

Citations for Bravery during the attacks on the towns of Visselhövede on the 19th of April 1945, and Zeven on the 24th April 1945

No. 2663510 CORPORAL (LANCE-SERGEANT) SAMUEL VINEY (Military Medal)

On the 19th April, 1945, this Battalion carried out an attack on the town of Visselhövede. This N.C.O. was commanding one of the leading sections ordered to clear up the main road leading out of the town to the north. As his section reached this road they came under heavy automatic fire, wounding some and forcing the remainder to cover. This N.C.O. immediately reorganized his depleted command, dragged the wounded men from the road back to cover and then immediately led on to clear the nearest post obstructing his advance. In this he was successful and the momentum of the company attack was thus never allowed to diminish.

During the whole of this time this N.C.O. had been operating under heavy and accurate small-arms fire and there is no doubt that it was due to his utter disregard of his own safety and great power of leadership that the above satisfactory results were achieved. This N.C.O. has invariably behaved in this outstanding way in action and his example has at all times been an inspiration to his section and indeed the whole platoon.

W.S./Lieutenant JOHN GREVILL B CHESTER 1 Company (Military Cross)

On 24th April, 1945, this officer was commanding the forward platoon of the right forward company in the Battalion attack on Zeven. His first task was to take his platoon forward to gain the first objective before the rest of the Battalion moved and he had to remain there alone for three-quarters of an hour exposed to heavy mortar and machine-gun fire while a neighbouring battalion came up alongside. When once a further advance was permitted this officer's platoon led the company attack across a long stretch of open ground to the next objective. En-route his leading section all became casualties, but Lieutenant Chester immediately himself picked up the Bren and led the remains of his platoon into the strongly held wood which formed this objective. Here due to his great bravery and power of leadership the attack never paused for an instant, and despite further losses Lieutenant Chester led on into the town itself and ultimately reached his final objective on the other side of it. There is no doubt that the very fine performance of this company was largely due to this officer's entire disregard of his own personal safety and great devotion to duty throughout the long and arduous battle, of which he personally bore the full brunt. It was thanks to him that the whole Battalion attack was able to keep up its momentum and to achieve complete success.

ADDENDUM IV

The Rhineland battlefields then and now

The Treaty of Versailles, signed in July 1919, eight months after WW1 decreed that the Rhineland was to be demilitarized. Adolf Hitler seized full power in Germany in 1933. Work on the Siegfried Line began soon after and continued throughout the 1930s. It saw the development of the fortifications from the Swiss border to as far north as Nijmegen, over 400 miles, and featured more than 18,000 bunkers, tunnels and tank traps. However, at the start of WW2 the defences remained incomplete and as Germany was on the offensive it remained unfinished until work restarted after the D Day invasion. 20,000 forced labourers, locals, and the *'Reich Labour Service'*, worked to try and complete the defences, mostly building anti-tank ditches. German propaganda, both at home and abroad, repeatedly portrayed the Siegfried Line during its construction as an unbreachable bulwark.

In the area of ground fought over during Operation

Veritable and Blockbuster, the Siegfried Line was largely under used, instead the defending troops tending to fight from houses, farms, and trenched and sandbagged fortifications. The Siegfried line was made most effective by the Germans' flooding of the area, which presented a formidable barrier for the allied attack; preventing movement of armoured vehicles and very effectively totally blocking the American advance across the Roer river for weeks, enabling the defenders to concentrate their resources towards the British and Canadian advance.

It is widely understood that the German forces were largely 'spent' after Normandy and the battle of the bulge. That was true for some of the fighting troops who were made up of poorly trained and equipped youths and elderly men. Certainly only low numbers of panzer units were on the battleground, although they were used very effectively and more than a match for all but the 'Firefly Sherman tanks' with their larger gun. However, the German Parachute Army under General Schelm was very well resourced and backed up with more than sufficient numbers of artillery pieces and self-propelled guns to cause significant problems to the advancing troops. The parachutists were extremely well led and highly motivated troops. Some may have been fanatical nazis, but all were fighting for their homeland and all had the knowledge that they were under orders to fight to the last man. The British and Canadian troops had almost infinite supplies of vehicles and firepower, including aircraft. The huge air raids on Kleve and Goch alone totally destroyed the cities from the outset of Operation Veritable. This cocktail meant that the fighting was bitter and the destruction of epic proportions. After the war, Eisenhower commented this "was some of the fiercest fighting of the whole war" and "a bitter slugging match in which the enemy had to be forced back yard by yard". Montgomery wrote "the enemy parachute troops fought with a fanaticism un-excelled at any time in the war" and "the volume of fire from enemy weapons was the heaviest which had so far been met by British troops in the campaign."

In the 31 days of Operation Veritable and Blockbuster, the cost to the British and Canadian forces involved amounted to 15,600 dead or wounded. Operation Grenade (the American part of the 'pincer movement') cost them 7,300 casualties. It must have been worse still for the German defenders who had no reserves, and yet bravely and skilfully defended ground to the last man. Their forces lost 22,000 dead or wounded and a further 22,000 taken as prisoners of war. Nevertheless, they had put up a heroic effort against overwhelming forces, had in many instances fought to the last man, had slowed the planned advance by some 27 days, and made the allies pay a huge price for their victory. The 5th Battalion Coldstream, and indeed the whole of the Guards Armoured Division had faced the toughest and most sustained fighting of the war under unimaginable conditions.

Today, despite the destruction, there are still traces of the Siegfried line, particularly within the Reichswald Forest. There are numerous concrete bunkers, most having been severely damaged in the fighting. For the most part the land has been returned to farming or developed as new housing. Only a few buildings that sustained repairable damage exist, most were completely rebuilt after the war. The towns of Kleve and Goch have all been almost completely rebuilt.

The wartime maps used gridlines that do not correspond to modern maps thus the six-digit map coordinates routinely referred to in war diaries make no sense when trying to locate them on modern maps. There is an excellent online resource that can translate these coordinates.

www.echodelta.net/mbs/eng-welcome.php

Use this to find the two letter code for the area you are looking for and then (for northern Europe) select 'Nord de Guerre Zone' from the drop down menu in the 'Coordinates translator'. Enter the two letter code followed by the six digit map reference from the war diary. Example for Metzekath rA095325

Recommended battlefield sights:

1.   Viller Mühle and surrounding farms near
        Hommersum
This place was also mentioned in the war diary. You can see clear bullet holes. Heavy fighting must have taken place here.

Google: https://goo.gl/maps/SHnurpQuKJTghNXA9
Wikipedia: https://de.wikipedia.org/wiki/Viller_M%C3%BCChle

2.   Bunker of the Siegfried line south of Goch
The bunker can be seen from the highway in a private garden. The owner may allow access into his garden. The bunker is blown up from the inside, the entrances are bricked up. In

the meadow behind the farm there are traces of a tank ditch used now for drainage. The bunker has no traces of fighting.

Google: https://goo.gl/maps/TdVUXBeiLS2WGvUk9

3.   Bunker of the Siegfried line west of Goch,
         Hassumer Straße
This bunker is very hidden on private property. It is built similarly to the first bunker and is very overgrown and hard to see.

Google: https://goo.gl/maps/dNzt1jbRFbX9TFy76

4.   Bunker of the Siegfried line north of Goch in Kessel
Another bunker of the Siegfried Line. Here, too, there are no traces of fighting.

Google: https://goo.gl/maps/6MFovc2AV1JpYUa17

5.   Reichswald British War cemetery
This British war cemetery is the largest in Germany with 7600 fallen soldiers. A very quiet and honourable place that makes you think.

Google: https://goo.gl/maps/7rpeqcuANgV7LjxW6
Wikipedia: https://de.wikipedia.org/wiki/Reichswald_Forest_ War_Cemetery

6.   Groesbeek Canadian War cemetery
This war graves cemetery is located on a hill north of Groesbeek. In daylight, you have a clear view over Groesbeek

and the Reichswald Forest. In the Netherlands, the allies are especially remembered as liberators. There is a tradition that a candle is placed on every single war grave throughout the Netherlands every year on Christmas Eve, creating an emotional atmosphere when everything is lit up in candlelight.

Google: https://goo.gl/maps/Le2x9vkXdJ7MANmr
Wikipedia   https://en.wikipedia.org/wiki/Groesbeek_
                      Canadian_War_Cemetery

7.   Trenches in the Reichswald
Some of the trenches are clearly visible, some being quite deep

Google: https://goo.gl/maps/SUoraVkoQbzcghNXA

8.   Mooshof Uedem – Story of Aubrey Cosens
http://vconline.org.uk/aubrey-cosens-vc/4586261539

Google: https://goo.gl/maps/76Vd5FgNgFppqi4Z7

9.   Railroad bridge Wesel
The most important destination for crossing the Rhine. It was blown up by German troops in March 1945 and never rebuilt

Google: https://goo.gl/maps/tMzWWDXFbgybi5Q57

10.   Waco Glider
The Waco CG-4 is an American military glider that was frequently used during Operation Market Garden. Hundreds

of Gliders landed in Groesbeek and the surrounding area during the operation in September 1944. September 2014 marked the 70th anniversary of Operation Market Garden. This has been grandly commemorated in Groesbeek and the surrounding area. On September 17, 2014, soldiers of the U.S. 82nd Division unveiled a memorial at Klein-America. In addition to the life-size Waco glider, an information column was placed. On it you can see movies about the Second World War and the Waco Glider.

Google: https://goo.gl/maps/a1vp9MK8snVqvTuP8

11.   Muna Xanten

Ammunition depot in the 2nd world war. Muna Xanten was an ammunition facility of the German Air Force. It was responsible not only for the production of munitions, but also for "the recovery, analysis and defusing of enemy munitions dropped on Germany". On November 20, 1942, an explosion occurred in Workhouse 4 during the assembly of a B-1000 aerial mine, causing the death of 43 people (1 fireman, 40 labourers, 2 women workers). To commemorate the victims of the disaster, a monument was erected opposite the site of the accident after the war. Walking through this forest you will see hundreds of destroyed bunkers. The depot was top secret and nobody in Xanten knew about it.

Google: https://goo.gl/maps/tI IZGyfdhiJfCY98VA
Wikipedia: Luftmunitionsanstalt Xanten – Wikipedia

12. Memorial in Bönninghardt
Google: https://goo.gl/maps/7pywrushBRFn3GGJ

ADDENDUM V

Retracing Basil's steps

Basil arrived in Ostend on or around the 6th of January 1945. *(See chapter 7)* He stayed at 'Au Petit Bateau', 6 Avenue de Smet de Nayer. The street was extensively rebuilt in the 1990s but to the same layout. Number 6 still exists but is now a completely new block of flats. The foyer of the flats next door contains photographs of how the street looked just prior to the outbreak of WW2.

'Au Petit Bateau' was a pretty little hotel, set in a four story stone and brick elegant façade that curved with the shallow corner it was set in. The frontage proudly displayed the Belgian flag, with AU PETIT BATEAU in large letters spanning the whole frontage. The ground floor had a central entrance door with windows either side displaying CAFÉ – RESTAURANT on the left and PENSION – HOTEL to the right. The upper floors were used as the guest rooms. There were similar hotels either side of it.

The Belgian villages of Neerlissem and Opheylissum, now collectively known as a' Helecine, suffered no war damage and consequently have changed very little. The Chateau remains a beautiful building and is open to the public for walks and children's play areas, with a café in the grounds. *(See chapter 7)*

Close by is a museum of Village Life – *Musée communal Armand Pellegrin*. The museum has a copy of a publication detailing visits by small groups of Coldstream Guards in July 1945 and again in September 1986. The publication is entitled Les Coldstream Guards a' Helecine. The July 1945 event involved a 'Commemoration of Victory' with a cortege of locals and a 40 strong delegation of Coldstream Guards.

The ground over which Basil's first attack was made across the sand dunes east of Gennep has changed very little. *(See chapter 11)* There are traces of trench lines in the position taken by 3 Company which may have been German or were dug by 3 Company. The area by the question mark shaped small lake that was Basil and 4 Company's objective is shown in the photograph below. This area is flat but the dunes between there and Gennep are surprisingly high and obvious as to why they presented such a difficult terrain for their carriers to negotiate with their supplies. From the edge of the dunes just to the right of the picture the flat ground up to and across the border into Germany can easily be seen.

The area by the question mark shaped small lake that was Basil and 4 Company's objective in his first attack.

To retrace Basil's route from his objective in the dunes by the small question mark shaped lake, to the start line for the attack on the Siegfried line at Müll, you walk or drive south-easterly along the gravelled *Zandkuilseweg* track, and onward along the now tarmacked *Kamperweg* road until almost to the E1 Autobahn. You pass Hommersum village just a few hundred yards away on the left *(See Chapter 12)*. The church tower is easily visible through the trees just beyond the river Kendel. The German border is to your left some 100 yards across a field. The start line for the attack is across that field as far as the *Mortelweg* Road, where it passes between the two farms. The centre line of the attack on Müll ran roughly parallel to the modern E1 autobahn with the river Kendel flanking their left and the autobahn service area to the right. Looking east from the start line, the houses seen in the distance through the trees are what remains of Müll. The old frontier post, the objective for 1 Company is just the other side of the autobahn.

View of Hommersum church tower and village across the German border – looking east from Kamperweg

The ferocity of the fighting during the attack on Müll, together with the flooding of the river Kendel have obliterated many of the original roads and tracks Basil would have seen. There are no signs of bullet or shell holes in the buildings that exist on the original footprints suggesting that they were totally rebuilt after the war. The river Kendel is now returned to a gentle and peaceful stream and the ground no longer waterlogged.

Buildings in Müll today, rebuilt after the devastation from the flooding and fighting in February 1945, that also caused the road layout to be dramatically changed.

At Buchholt *(see Chapter 13)*, all of the farm buildings have been rebuilt or repaired, some still showing clear damage from the intense shelling. The farm Basil was positioned by is called Kühnenhof Farm and predominantly farms pigs. Original bullet holes and explosion damage can still be clearly seen on the two barns.

Kühnenhof farm in Buchholt today where Basil and 4 Company were positioned. Many of the original bullet holes and explosion damage can still be seen on the two barns.

At Metzekath some of the buildings have been rebuilt and others added (See chapter 16). On the 23rd of March 1945 a recognisance flight captured images of Metzekath showing clear evidence of the multiple shell craters made by the bombardment at the start of the attack. Most of the craters are around the farm buildings that Basil and 4 Company attacked and captured on that bloody day. To this day there are still the tell-tale signs of battle on those farm buildings. The walls are peppered with bullet holes and shell holes, the repairs failing to hide the indelibly marked violence. The woods surrounding Metzekath are still mostly of the same layout as when Basil saw them and contain some craters from shells. The open ground between the woods and the farm that was so heavily contested remains the same.

In recent times the local 'Rheinische Post' newspaper reported on a new building with a restaurant and boarding house on the site. It provided some useful information on the history of the Metzekath site after the attack on the 5th of March 1945. It reported that the buildings were badly damaged by shell fire but in the latter stages of the war the buildings were taken over and used as a military hospital, the residents being evacuated to Kevelaer. For some time after the war the destroyed German artillery guns remained as they had been positioned on the 5th March 1945 as a monument to the large numbers on both sides who died during the battle.

In the late 1990s the farmer had found large quantities of ammunition and two bodies whilst digging out a pond on the site where it is believed the trenched position had been.

At Haus Loo (see chapter 17) the battlefield that lays between the railway embankment and the Xanten – Rheinberg road has changed very little in that the open ground overlooking Haus Loo is still flat pasture, the rail tracks remain but are now disused, and the view from the top of the rail embankment would be as seen back in March 1945. Some new housing development has taken place particularly to the left of the battlefield. Of the older houses that were in place during the battle, there are no obvious signs of war damage due to walls being rendered or otherwise repaired. At the objective where Basil and 4 Company reached on the 9th of March 1945 there can still be seen a tunnel under the rail track where at least some of them would have been able to avoid the heavy shell, mortar, and nebelwerfer fire.

Views of Metzekath today. Damage to the walls caused during the attack on 5th March 1945 is still visible

View towards Metzekath of the upward sloping ground from the tree line. The main gun emplacement that was overrun was sighted on the extreme left of the picture.

The walls on one or two buildings on the Xanten – Rheinberg Road contain the tell-tale signs of repaired war damage.

The damage to Haus Loo has been completely repaired from the violence of the battle. The majority of the damage was to the cow sheds to the rear and at least one shell hole through the wall of one of the rear bedrooms. The medieval earthworks in front of Haus Loo have a shell battered appearance.

The tunnel at the point on the rail track that was Basil and 4 Company's objective

View towards the Zanten – Rheinberg road from the point on the rail track that was Basil and 4 Company's objective

View of the front of Haus Loo today with no sign of the damage from the fighting in March 1945. The front of the building actually received remarkably little damage as it faced away from the direction of attack.

*View of the open ground between where the attack took place
and Haus Loo*

*Tranquil view from the side of Haus Loo looking across the battlefield
from roughly where one of the 88mm artillery guns was sighted. The
attack came from left to right across the green field. The medieval moated
area that bore the brunt of the attack is off to the left of the picture.*

View of part of the cellar under Haus Loo where Erika Bremer and her family hid throughout the fighting

View of only a small area of the Reichswald forest cemetery containing some of the fallen from the attack on Haus Loo

Most of those of the 5th Battalion that were killed in action were initially buried in the field beside Haus Loo over which they attacked. They were later re-buried at the Reichswald forest cemetery.

The Wesel Rail bridge was never repaired and remains there as a giant silent monument to the achievements of Basil and all the boys of the 5th Battalion.

View of the badly damaged brick Rail Bridge ramp at Wesel, the steel structure spanning the river was blown up by the retreating Germans just after the successful attack at Haus Loo. The 5th Battalion's capture of the Xanten to Rheinberg Road left them with no choice but to retreat across the Rhine and destroy the road and rail bridges.

ADDENDUM VI

Composition of 21st Army Group 1945

Composition of 21st Army Group 1945	
1st Canadian Army	II Canadian Corps + multi-national forces
2nd British Army	I Corps – not active in Operations Veritable and Blockbuster but various Brigades and Regiments loaned to XXX Corps
	XII Corps – not active in Operations Veritable and Blockbuster but various Brigades and Regiments loaned to XXX Corps
	XXX Corps

Composition of II CANADIAN CORPS 1945		
2nd Can. Infantry Division	Machine Gun	Toronto Scottish Regiment
	Reconnaissance	14th Canadian Hussars
	4th Infantry Brigade	Royal Regiment of Canada
		Essex Scottish Regiment
		Royal Hamilton Light Infantry
	5th Infantry Brigade	Black Watch of Canada
		Regiment de Maisonneuve
		Calgary Highlanders
	6th Infantry Brigade	Fusiliers Mont Royal
		Queens Own Cameron
		Highlanders of Canada
		South Saskatchewan Regiment
	Royal Canadian Artillery	4th Field Regiment
		2nd, 14th, 26th Field Battery
		5th, 6th Field Regiment
		5th, 13th, 28th, 73rd Field Battery
		21st, 91st Field Battery
		2nd Anti-Tank Regiment
		18th, 20th 23rd, 108th Tank Battery
		3rd Light Anti-Aircraft Regt
		16th, 17th, Light Anti-Aircraft Battery
		38th Light Anti-Aircraft Battery
	Royal Canadian Engineers	1st, 2nd, 7th, 11th Field Park Company, one bridging platoon
	Royal Canadian Signals	2nd Canadian Divisional Signals
	Royal Canadian Army Service Corps	4th, 5th, 6th, Infantry Brigade Company
2nd Can. Infantry Division		Second Infantry Divisional Troops Company

		No. 2 Infantry Division Ordnance Field Park
	Royal Canadian Army Medical Corps	
	RCEME	4th, 5th, 6th, Infantry Brigade Workshop
3rd Can. Infantry Division	Reconnaissance	7th Canadian Regiment
	7th Can. Infantry Brigade	The Royal Winnipeg Rifles
		The Regina Rifles Regiment
		1st Battalion Canadian Scottish Regiment
	8th Can. Infantry Brigade	The Queen's Own Rifles
		The North Shore Regiment
		Régiment de la Chaudière
	9th Can. Infantry Brigade	The Stormont, Dundas & Glengarry Highlanders
		The North Nova Scotia Highlanders
		The Cameron Highlanders of Ottawa
	2nd Can. Armoured Brigade	10th Can. Armoured Regiment (The Fort Garry Horse)
		27th Can. Armoured Regiment (The Sherbrooke Regiment)
	Royal Canadian Artillery	12th 13th 14th 19th Can. Field Regs
		12th Canadian LAD
		3rd Anti-Tank Regiment
		62nd Anti-Tank Regiment
		80th Anti-Aircraft Brigade
		4th Canadian Light Anti-Aircraft Regiment

	Royal Canadian Engineers	-
	4th Special Service Brig.	No. 48 (Royal Marine) Commando
		Royal Canadian Medical Corps
4th Can. Armoured Division	HQ Division	10th Infantry Brigade Ground Defence Platoon
		29th Armoured Reconnaissance Regiment (The South Alberta)
	4th Can. Armoured Brigade	21st Armoured Regiment (The Governor General's Foot Guards)
		22nd Armoured Regiment (The Grenadier Guards)
		28th Armoured Regiment (The British Columbia Regiment)
		The Lake Superior Regiment (Motor)
	10th Can. Infantry Brigade	10th Independent Machine Gun Company (New Brunswick Rangers)
		The Lincoln and Welland Regiment
		The Algonquin Regiment
		The Argyll and Sutherland Highlanders
	Royal Can. Artillery	15th Field Regiment
		23rd Field Regiment
		5th Anti-tank Regiment
		8th Light Anti-aircraft Regiment
	Royal Can. Engineers	HQ Squadrons
	Royal Can. Signals	4th Armoured Divisional Signals
	Royal Can. Service Corps	HQ Companies
	Royal Can. Medical Corps	-

	Royal Can. Ordinance Co.	No. 4 Armoured Division Ordnance
	RCEME HQ	RCEME

Composition of XXX CORPS 1945		
43rd Wessex Division	Armoured Reconnaissance	43rd Reconnaissance Reg
	214th Infantry Brigade	5th Battalion, Duke of Cornwall's Light Infantry
		7th Battalion, Somerset Light Infantry
		9th Battalion, Somerset Light Infantry
		1st Battalion, Worcestershire Regiment
	129th Infantry Brigade	4th Battalion, Somerset Light Infantry
		4th Battalion, Wiltshire Regiment
		5th Battalion, Wiltshire Regiment
	130th Infantry Brigade	4th Battalion, Dorset Regiment
		7th Battalion, Hampshire Regiment
		5th Battalion, Dorset Regiment
	Machine Gun	8th Bat Middlesex Reg
	Royal Artillery	94th Field Regiment
		112th Field Regiment
		179th Field Regiment
		59th Anti-Tank Regiment
		110th Light Anti-Aircraft Regiment
	Royal Signals	43rd Divisional Signals
	Royal Engineers	204th Field Company
		260th Field Company
		553rd Field Company
		207th Field Park Company
		13th Bridging Platoon

52nd Lowland Division (Initially under command of XII Corps)	155th Infantry Brigade	7th/9th Battalion, Royal Scots Fusiliers
		4th Battalion, King's Own Scottish Borderers
		6th Battalion, Highland Light Infantry (from 12 February 1945)
	156th Infantry Brigade	**4th/5th Battalion, Royal Scots Fusiliers**
		6th Battalion, Cameronians (Scottish Rifles)
		7th Battalion, Cameronians (Scottish Rifles) (left 13 March 1945)
		1st Battalion, Glasgow Highlanders (from 14 March 1945)
	157th Infantry Brigade	1st Battalion, Glasgow Highlanders (left 12 March 1945)
		5th Battalion, Highland Light Infantry
		6th Battalion, Highland Light Infantry (left 12 February 1945)
		5th Battalion, King's Own Scottish Borderers (from 12 February 1945)
		7th Battalion, Cameronians (Scottish Rifles) (from 14 March 1945)
	52nd Divisional artillery, Royal Artillery	79th (Lowland) Field Regiment
		80th (Lowland – City of Glasgow) Field Regiment
		186th Field Regiment
		1st Mountain Regiment (until 21 March 1945)
		54th (Queen's Own Royal Glasgow Yeomanry) Anti-Tank Regiment
		108th Light Anti-Aircraft Regiment

	52nd Divisional engineers, Royal Engineers	241st (Lowland) Field Company
		554th Field Company
		202nd (East Lancashire) Field Company
		243rd (Lowland) Field Park Company, Royal Engineers
		17th Bridging Platoon
	Royal Corps of Signals	52nd Divisional Signals
	Machine Gun Battalion	7th Battalion, Manchester Regiment
	Royal Armoured Corps	52nd Reconnaissance Regiment
51st Highland Division	152nd Infantry Brigade	2nd Bat, The Seaforth Highlanders
		5th Bat, The Seaforth Highlanders
		5th Bat, The Queen's Own Cameron Highlanders
	153rd Infantry Brigade	5th Battalion, The Black Watch
		1/5/7th Battalions The Gordon Highlanders
	154th Infantry Brigade	1st Battalion, The Black Watch
		7th (Fife) Battalion, The Black Watch
		7th Battalion, The Argyll and Sutherland Highlanders
	Support	1st/7th Bat, The Mid'sex Regiment
	Royal Armoured Corps	2nd Derbyshire Yeomanry,
	Royal Artillery	126th Field Regiment
		127th Field Regiment
		128th Field Regiment
		61st Anti-Tank Regiment
	Royal Engineers	274th Field Company
		275th Field Company

		276th Field Company
		10th Bridging Platoon
53rd Welsh Infantry Division	34th Armoured Brigade	107th Regiment Royal Arm'd Corps
		147th Regiment Royal Arm'd Corps
		7th Royal Tank Regiment
		9th Royal Tank Regiment
	8th Armoured Brigade (Initially under command of XII Corps)	Sherwood Rangers Yeomanry
		4th/7th Royal Dragoon Guards
		13th/18th Royal Hussars
		12th (Queen's Westminsters) Battalion, King's Royal Rifle Corps
	158th Infantry Brigade	7th Battalion, Royal Welch Fusiliers
		1/5th Battalion, Welch Regiment
		1st Battalion, East Lancashire Reg
	160th Infantry Brigade	4th Battalion, Welch Regiment
		2nd Battalion, Monmouthshire Reg
		6th Battalion, Royal Welch Fusiliers
	71st Infantry Brigade	1st Battalion, Oxfordshire and Buckinghamshire Light Infantry
		1st Battalion, Highland Light Infantry
		4th Battalion, Royal Welch Fusiliers
	Royal Artillery	53rd Divisional Artillery
		81st (Welsh) Field Regiment
		83rd Field Regiment
		133rd Field Regiment
		71st (Royal Welch Fusiliers) Anti-Tank Regiment
		25th Light Anti-Aircraft Regiment
	Royal Engineers	53rd Divisional Engineers
		244th (Welsh) Field Company
53rd Welsh Infantry Division		282nd Field Company

		555th Field Company
		285th Field Park Company
		22nd Bridging Platoon
	Royal Signals	53rd (Welsh) Divisional Signals Regiment, Royal Corps of Signals
	Machine Gun	1st Machine Gun Battalion
	Reconnaissance	53rd Recce Regiment, Royal Armoured Corps
3rd Infantry Division (Initially under command of XII Corps)	8th Infantry Brigade HQ	8th Infantry Brigade
		Signal Section & Light Aid Detachment 1st Bn. The Suffolk Regt.
		2nd Bn. The East Yorkshire Regiment
		1st Bn. The South Lancashire Regt.
	9th Infantry Brigade	9th Infantry Brigade HQ Signal Section & Light Aid Detachment
		2nd Bn. The Lincolnshire Regiment
		1st Bn. The King's Own Scottish Borderers
		2nd Bn. The Royal Ulster Rifle
	185th Infantry Brigade	Headquarters, Signal Section & Light Aid Detachment
		2nd Bn. The Royal Warwickshire Regt.
		1st Bn. The Royal Norfolk Regiment
		2nd Bn. The King's Shropshire L. Infantry
	Divisional Troops	3rd Reconnaissance Reg't, Royal Armoured Corps
		2nd Bn. The Middlesex Regiment
	Royal Artillery	3rd Infantry Divisional HQ
		7th Field Regiment (9th, 16th & 17th/43rd Field Batteries
		33rd Field Regiment, (H.Q., 101st/109th & 113th/114th Field Batteries)
		76th (Highland) Field Regiment
		20th Anti-Tank Regiment

		92nd Light Anti-Aircraft Regiment
	Royal Engineers	3rd Infantry Divisional HQ
		17th Field Company
		246th (Welsh) Field Company
		253rd (West Lancashire) Field Company
		15th Field Park Company
		2nd Bridging Platoon
	Royal Corps of Signals	3rd Divisional Signals
	Royal Army Service Corps	3rd Infantry Divisional HQ
		23rd Company
		47th Company
		48th Company
		172nd Company
	Royal Army Medic Corps	-
	REME	-
11th Armoured Division	29th Armoured Brigade	23rd Hussars
		2nd Fife and Forfar Yeoman
		3rd Royal Tank Regiment
		8th Bat, Rifle Brigade
	159th Infantry Brigade	4th Bat, K's Shropshire Light Infantry
		3rd Bat, Monmouthshire Regiment
		1st Bat, Herefordshire Regiment
	Divisional Troops	2nd Independent Machine Gun Co.
		15th/19th The K's Royal Hussars
	Royal Artillery	13th Regiment, Royal Horse Artillery
		58th (Argyll and Sutherland Highlanders) Light Anti-Aircraft Regiment
	Royal Engineers	13th Field Squadron,
		612th Field Squadron
		147th Field Park Squadron

	Royal Signals	11th Armoured Divisional Regiment
Guards Armoured Division	Arm'd Reconnaissance	2nd Bat Welsh Guards
	5th Guards Armoured Brig	1st Bat Grenadier Guards
		2nd Bat Grenadier Guards
		1st Bat Coldstream Guards
		2nd Bat Irish Guards
	32nd Guards Brigade	**5th Bat Coldstream Guards**
		3rd Bat Irish Guards
		1st Bat Welsh Guards
		No.1 Machine Gun Co. (Northumberland Fusiliers)
	Royal Artillery	153rd Field Regiment
		55th Field Regiment
		21st Anti-tank Regiment
		94th Light Anti-aircraft Reg
	Royal Engineers	14th Field Squadron
		615th Field Squadron
		148th Field Squadron
		11th Bridging Troop
	Royal Signals	Guards Armoured Div Signals
	Royal Army Service Corps	-
	Royal Army Medical Corps	19th Light Field Ambulance
		128th Field Ambulance
	Royal Army Ord. Corps	-
	REME	-
Independent	6th Guards Armoured Brig	4th Battalion Coldstream Guards
		4th Battalion Grenadier Guards
		3rd Tank Battalion Scots Guards

Every effort has been made to ensure that this is a definitive list but it's completeness cannot be confirmed

ADDENDUM VII

Timeline for Operation Veritable and Blockbuster

Date	Day	Event
8.2.45	1	Launch of Operation Veritable. 3rd Can. Div. clear villages in floods north of Reichswald Forest. 15th Scottish Div. advance north of Reichswald Forest towards Kleve. 2nd Can. Div. advance behind 15th Scottish Div. 53rd Welsh Div. advance into Reichswald Forest. 51st Highland Div. advance southeast into Reichswald Forest towards Goch. 43rd Wessex and Guards Armoured Div. held in reserve.
9.2.45	2	Matterhorn feature near Kleve captured by 15th Scottish Div. 53rd Welsh Div. capture high ground in Reichswald Forest. 2nd Canadian Div. meet heavy resistance and temporarily withdraw. 51st Highland Div. capture southern part of Reichswald Forest and cross Gennep Road south of Forest. Progress slowing due to atrocious weather and ground conditions. 43rd Wessex advance towards Kleve and enter huge traffic jam together with 15th Scottish Div. US 9th Army unable to cross Roer river as planned due to floods.

10.2.45	3	43rd Wessex skirt around Kleve and stop south of the town whilst town cleared. Traffic jam still holding up any further advances. German troops reinforcing rapidly. Rising floods north of forest now 4 feet deep.
11.2.45	4	Kleve finally captured.
12.2.45	5	German 47 Panzer Corps (116th Panzer Div. and 15th Panzer Div.) counterattack northwards towards Reichswald Forest between Kleve and Goch. Eventually repulsed and form a defensive line between Gennep and Kleve with support of 80th Infantry Corps (84th Infantry and 6th and 7th Parachutists). 51st Highland Div. capture Gennep and Hekkens. 43rd Wessex Div. and 15th Scottish Div. advance south of Kleve whilst 3rd Canadian Div. advance southwest through flooded area between Kleve and Rhine.
13.2.45	6	43rd Wessex Div. begin attack from south of Kleve towards Goch. 53rd Welsh Div. finally capture Reichswald Forest.
14.2.45	7	Weather cleared to allow Typhoon rocket attacks. 43rd Wessex make slow progress south towards Goch, facing fierce resistance. 32nd Guards Brigade (including 5th **Battalion Coldstream Guards**) of the Guards Armoured Division join 51st Highland Division to attack eastwards from Gennep towards Goch.
15.2.45	8	43rd Wessex continue to make slow progress south towards Goch.
16.2.45	9	32nd Guards Brigade (including 5th **Battalion Coldstream Guards**) of the Guards Armoured Division with 51st Highland Division continue attack eastwards into the Siegfried Line towards Goch. 43rd Wessex close in on Goch.
17.2.45	10	43rd Wessex cut Goch to Kalkar Road.
18.2.45	11	52nd Lowland Div. join the attack and push east towards Goch but halted for several days.
18.2.45	12	43rd Wessex battle for Goch.
20.2.45	13	43rd Wessex battle for Goch. 2nd Canadian Div. re-join the advance north of Kleve and advance towards Kalkar in waterlogged conditions

21.2.45	14	43rd Wessex finally capture Goch. 2nd Canadian Div attack Moyland Wood.
22.2.45	15	2nd Canadian Div. cross Goch to Kalkar Road.
23.2.45	16	Operation Grenade launched by US 9th Army across River Roer. 5th Armoured Brigade of Guards Armoured Div. (including 5th **Battalion Coldstream Guards**) secure Goch to Kalkar Road.
24.2.45	17	US 9th Army advance rapidly north towards Wesel Bridges on the Rhine.
25.2.45	18	US 9th Army near Alpen and Rheinberg
26.2.45	19	Launch of Operation Blockbuster. 2nd and 3rd Canadian Div. and 4th Canadian Armoured Div. attack through Guards Armoured Div. towards Xanten via the Hockwald Gap. 11th Armoured Div. attack through Guards Armoured Div. south towards Sonsbeck. 43rd Wessex attack along flooded area beside the Rhine towards Xanten. Keppeln, Kalkar and Uedem captured.
27.2.45	20	3rd Infantry Div. newly into battle attack southeast towards Wesel passing east of Kevelaer. Germans begin to withdraw to form bridgehead in front of the bridges at Wesel. 52nd Lowland Div. and 53rd Welsh Div. attack south towards Geldern. 4th Canadian Armoured Div. attack on Hockwald Gap temporarily suspended with heavy losses.
28.2.45	21	4th Canadian Armoured Div. renew attack on Hock-wald Gap.
1.3.45	22	Kervenheim captured by 3rd Infantry Division
2.3.45	23	53rd Welsh Div. capture Weeze.
3.3.45	24	53rd Welsh Div. capture Kevelaer (8th Armoured Brigade with 1st Battalion Ox and Bucks Light Infantry, with 4th/7th Royal Dragoon Guards) 53rd Welsh Div. meet US 9th Army at Geldern.

4.3.45	25	Guards Armoured Division (including **5th Battalion Coldstream Guards**) pass through Kevelaer and 3rd Infantry Div. east of Kapellen and attack the Bonninghardt Ridge on 5.3.45, reducing the German bridgehead.
5.3.45	26	43rd Wessex Div. and II Canadian Corps attack Xanten. **5th Battalion Coldstream Guards capture Metzekath**
6.3.45	27	3rd Canadian Div. attack Sonsbeck from the north. 3rd Infantry Div. attack Sonsbeck from the south.
7.3.45	28	Guards Armoured Division capture whole of Bonninghardt Ridge.
9.3.45	29	52nd Lowland Division attack the German Bridgehead and capture Haus Loo. Guards Armoured Division (including **5th Battalion Coldstream Guards**) attack the German Bridgehead and capture the Xanten to Rheinberg Road at Haus Loo, which was the last lateral supply route for German forces, making their position untenable. Xanten captured by the 5th Infantry Brigade of the 2nd Canadian Division. Alpen, Veen captured by 52nd Lowland Division Rheinberg captured by American forces
10.3.45	30	German forces retreat across the Rhine and blow the Wesel Bridges.

Acknowledgements

The primary source of the research for 'Our Boy' came from the 5th Battalion War Diary. This, coupled with Basil's soldier's paybook that detailed joining date and privilege leave dates gave confirmation that he was where the war diary stated. Most importantly the addresses on Basil's letters home gave proof of him being in 4 Company of the 5th Battalion which at first was in doubt as two months before he died, he had been transferred to the 1st Battalion.

My Mother – Iris, in particular, and my Auntie Vera also provided memories of Basil and life at home during the war years. Their memories often sent me off to research and confirm what they had stated. In all cases their memories were completely accurate.

Online research discovered all manner of video and photographic evidence of significant events such as the liberation of Dutch town of Enschede, the Rhine crossings, and Belsen concentration camp. In addition, the Imperial War Museum (IWM) and the Holocaust Museum in Washington have been consulted. A useful resource to assist with the comprehension of the magnitude of Operations

Veritable and Blockbuster was the You Tube series of three documentaries entitled the 'The battle for the Rhineland'.

Life in training camp at Caterham and Pirbright was provided with thanks from the late Guardsman Derrick Jackson who provided an excellent account of his training experience, courtesy of Ron Taylor.

The greatest lift to the research came from Svenja Wey-Peiricks who lives in the area where Operation Veritable and Blockbuster were fought. She visited all the battlefield sites Basil had fought in during February and March 1945 and provided photographs of damage to the buildings and structures that are still visible today. Her local knowledge was invaluable. Her grandparents actually lived yards from the very spot where Basil fought in March 1945 when involved in the attack on the Wesel bridgehead at Haus Loo. She even took the trouble to introduce me to the current owners of Haus Loo to gain historical information relevant to my research. Her enthusiasm went a long way to encourage my efforts to write the book and I cannot thank her enough for her contribution. My thanks also go to her husband Sebastian who together with Svenja provided a detailed guided tour of the battlefield sites for my brother and I in March 2022.

Thank you also to Pamela Mitchell who proof read an early copy of the draft and gave encouragement to pursue the book to its conclusion.

I must of course mention my sincere thanks to my wife Beverley for her patience and understanding during the many hours it took to research and write this book. Finally my thanks to my daughter Aimee for her help in correcting my spelling and grammar.

Although not directly quoted from, the following books,

papers, and web-based resources collectively provided an excellent means of gaining an insight into the daily life of a guardsman within Basil's 5th Battalion, the Guards Armoured Division actions, and the general conduct of the war in Holland and north-west Germany throughout 1945:

Books and Papers

A Distant Drum -The story of the 5th Battalion Coldstream Guards 1944-5 – Captain Jocelyn Pereira

Second to None – The history of the Coldstream Guards – Julian Paget

The Story of the Guards Armoured Division – Cpt the Earl of Rosse & Col E.R. Hill

With The Jocks – A Soldier's Struggle for Europe 1944-45 – Peter White

2 SG from 'Scots Guards 1919-1955 – David Erskine

History of the 6th (Lanarkshire) Battalion Cameronians – John Cossar

Grandad's War – A.C. Reynolds

The Last Offensive – Charles B. MacDonald

Lion Rampant – The Memoirs of an Infantry Officer from D-Day to the Rhineland – Robert Woolacombe

Armoured Guardsman – A War Diary June 1944 – April 1945 – Robert Boscawen

Tank Action – An Armoured Troop Commander's War 1944-45 – David Render

An Englishman at War – The War Diaries of Stanley Christopherson DSO, MC 1939-45 – James Holland

So Few Got Through – With the Gordon Highlanders from Normandy to the Baltic – Martin Lindsay

The Devil's Own Luck – Pegasus Bridge to the Baltic 1944-45 – Denis Edwards

From Dunkirk to the Rhineland – Ronald W Thompson
Armageddon – The Battle for Germany 1944-5 – Max Hastings
'Rheinische Post' newspaper – local newspaper carrying article on
     Metzekath (courtesy of Svenja Wey-Peiricks)
Les Cashiers d'Helecine Vol 9. – Musée communal Armand
     Pellegrin – Musée de la pédagogie – Visits by Coldstream
     Guards to Opheylissem
The Times newspaper – article describing the attack on Haus Loo

Web based resources

www.bbc.co.uk/history – BBC – WW2 People's War – Irish Guards
     Held Prisoner – Thuine Near Lingen Germany – Thuine
     Prisoner of War Camp article by denglish re Gdsn Seamus
     Morris
www.bbc.co.uk/archive – BBC Archive homepage – BBC Archive
     – BBC Radio News reports etc.
www.paradata.org.uk – Pilot Thomas Joyce
www.tim-online.nrw.de – Map of Germany
www.tracesofwar.com – Operation Veritable/Blockbuster
www.users.ox.ac.uk – Cumnor village history
www.rcafassociation.ca – 403 Squadron RCAF – Weather reports
     over Holland and Germany
www.cwgc.org – The Commonwealth War Graves Commission
www.warfarehistorynetwork.com – Battle of the Reichswald: Allies
     Surge Toward the Rhine
www.royalscotskosbwardiaries.co.uk – 4th Bn KOSB   1944 45 –
     War Diaries for Royal Kings Own Scottish Borderers
www.withthejocks.blogspot.com – A Visit to the Battlefields of
     Peter White: The Battle for Haus Loo: 9th March 1945 (details
     a visit in 2003 to Haus Loo by unknown author who had read
     'With the Jocks')

https://www.britain-at-war.org.uk/ww2/Derrick_Jackson/index.
htm – Derrick Jackson's account of training at Caterham
Barracks. Courtesy of Ron Taylor

www.historyplace.com/worldwar2 – The History Place – Hitler
Youth: Hitler's Boy Soldiers 1939-1945

www.iwm.org.uk/collections – Imperial War Museum
photographic and media collection

www.wikipedia.org – multiple sites covering most Divisions,
Regiments, Battalions

www.deplate.be/nl – Photo : Graaf De Smet de Naeyerlaan | The
Plate (deplate.be) – Photograph of Le Petit Batteau

https://www.echodelta.net/mbs/grillesj/norddeguerre.htm – War
diary coordinate locator for use in conjunction with echodelta
translator website. (Courtesy of Thierry Arsicaud)

You Tube – series of three documentaries entitled the 'The battle
for the Rhineland'.

The following all courtesy of Svenja Wey-Peiricks:

https://digitalarchive.mcmaster.ca/islandora/object/macrepo%
3A69412 – Calcar (Kalcar)

www.loc.gov/resource/g6000m.gct00041/?sp=5&r=0.034,0.094,
1.197,0.476,0 – Library of Congress – Cleve

www.loc.gov/resource/g6000m.gct00041/?sp=4&r=-0.127,0.168,
1.096,0.436,0 – Library of Congress – Goch

www.loc.gov/resource/g6000m.gct00040/?sp=2&r=0.461,0.206,
0.779,0.31,0 – Library of Congress – Groesbeek

www.loc.gov/resource/g6000m.gct00040/?sp=3&r=0.673,0.123,
0.425,0.169,0 – Library of Congress – Gennep

www.battlefieldhistorian.com – Photos, Maps, and Documents

Photographic Acknowledgements

Modern photographs of Op Veritable battle sites – courtesy of Svenja Wey-Peiricks

Photograph of Mansel Godwin in Germany – courtesy of Neil Godwin (son)

Photograph of 'Basil standing at ease' – courtesy of Martin Harris

All other photographs – supplied from author's own collection

Quotations used in 'Our Boy'

5th Battalion War Diary and included sketch maps (Contains public sector information licensed under the Open Government Licence v3.0). Open Government Licence (nationalarchives.gov.uk) Can be viewed on – http://ww2talk.com/index.php?threads/war-diary-5th-battalion-coldstream-guards--jan-oct-1945.57783/

Personal message from General Horrocks (Contains public sector information licensed under the Open Government Licence v3.0). Open Government Licence (nationalarchives.gov.uk) Can be viewed on – http://ww2talk.com/index.php?threads/war-diary-5th-battalion-coldstream-guards--jan-oct-1945.57783/

"Fighting Fifths" Last Parade – as produced in Guards Armoured Division's newsletter entitled 'The News Guardian' (Contains public sector information licensed under the Open Government Licence v3.0). Open Government Licence (nationalarchives.gov.uk) Can be viewed on – http://ww2talk.com/index.php?threads/war-diary-5th-battalion-coldstream-guards--jan-oct-1945.57783/

Excerpts from 'Brussels Sprout'- the 5th Battalion's newsletter (Contains public sector information licensed under the

Open Government Licence v3.0). Open Government Licence (nationalarchives.gov.uk) Can be viewed on – http://ww2talk.com/index.php?threads/war-diary-5th-battalion-coldstream-guards--jan-oct-1945.57783/

5th Battalion Bravery Citations and Reports (Contains public sector information licensed under the Open Government Licence v3.0). Open Government Licence (nationalarchives.gov.uk) Can be viewed on – http://ww2talk.com/index.php?threads/war-diary-5th-battalion-coldstream-guards--jan-oct-1945.57783/

Farewell to Armour Parade – Guards Armoured Division – 9th June 1945 (Contains public sector information licensed under the Open Government Licence v3.0). Open Government Licence (nationalarchives.gov.uk) Can be viewed on – http://ww2talk.com/index.php?threads/war-diary-5th-battalion-coldstream-guards--jan-oct-1945.57783/

The News Guardian – July 12th 1945 – The Fighting Fifth's Last Parade (Contains public sector information licensed under the Open Government Licence v3.0). Open Government Licence (nationalarchives.gov.uk) Can be viewed on – http://ww2talk.com/index.php?threads/war-diary-5th-battalion-coldstream-guards--jan-oct-1945.57783/

Erika Bremer's account – later written and translated by Svenja Wey-Peiricks (converted from third hand to first hand account by author)

Niel Godwin talking of his father Mansel – by Neil Godwin